TRAINING GUIDE FOR NEW GERMAN SHEPHERD OWNERS

HISTORY, HEALTH AND FAMOUS GSD'S PLUS PUPPY TRAINING INCLUDING HOUSE, POTTY AND CRATE TRAINING, LEASH, RECALL AND SEPARATION ANXIETY.

HELEN SUTHERLAND

TWENTY DOGS PUBLISHING

© Copyright Twenty Dogs Publishing 2021 - All rights reserved.

The content contained within this book may not be reproduced, duplicated or transmitted without direct written permission from the author or the publisher.

Under no circumstances will any blame or legal responsibility be held against the publisher, or author, for any damages, reparation, or monetary loss due to the information contained within this book. Either directly or indirectly. You are responsible for your own choices, actions, and results.

Legal Notice:

This book is copyright protected. This book is only for personal use. You cannot amend, distribute, sell, use, quote or paraphrase any part, or the content within this book, without the consent of the author or publisher.

Disclaimer Notice:

Please note the information contained within this document is for educational and entertainment purposes only. All effort has been executed to present accurate, up to date, and reliable, complete information. No warranties of any kind are declared or implied. Readers acknowledge that the author is not engaging in the rendering of legal, financial, medical or professional advice. The content within this book has been derived from various sources. Please consult a licensed professional before attempting any techniques outlined in this book.

By reading this document, the reader agrees that under no circumstances is the author responsible for any losses, direct or indirect, which are incurred as a result of the use of the information contained within this document, including, but not limited to, errors, omissions, or inaccuracies.

Subtitle

The essential positive recall and leash training guide. Includes all the training cues including come, heel, sit, stay and the emergency stop

Author: Helen E. Sutherland

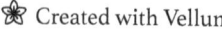 Created with Vellum

CONTENTS

INTRODUCTION	1
1. A BRIEF HISTORY OF GERMAN SHEPHERDS	5
Max Emil Friedrich von Stephanitz	6
The War	7
The Working Dog	8
2. TYPES AND LINES	10
The Show Line	11
American and Canadian Show Line	12
West German (European) Show Line	13
Working Line	13
West (German) Working Line	14
East German Working Line DDR	14
Czech Working Line	15
Pet Line	16
Variants	16
East-European Shepherd	16
King Shepherd	17
Shiloh Shepherd	18
White Shepherd	19
White Swiss Shepherd	20
Sable German Shepherd	20
3. HEALTH	21
Common illnesses	22
Hip & Elbow Dysplasia	23
Gastric Dilatation Volvulus (GDV) or Bloat	24
Elbow dysplasia	24
Canine Degenerative Myelopathy (DM)	25
Anal Furunculosis (Perianal Fistulae)	26
Eyes	27
Ears	29

4. HOW TO FIND A REPUTABLE BREEDER 31
   How to recognise a puppy farm 32
   Advertising 32
   The Seller 33

5. ARRIVING HOME 35
   What's in a name? 36
   He's home! 37
   Socialization 38
   Vaccinations over the first year 39

6. HOUSE AND POTTY TRAINING 41
   How long can a puppy wait for the toilet 42
   Puppy Pads 42
   How to manage their potty training 44
   Where? 44
   Supervise and be vigilant 45
   How to clean up the mess 46
   Create a Schedule 46
   Your schedule 46
   Sleep 47
   Bedtime 48

7. CRATE TRAINING 50
   Introducing your pup to the crate 51
   Size of Crate 54

8. FOOD AND FEEDING 56
   Diet and Weight 56
   What to feed him 56
   How much to feed 58
   What not to feed - dangerous foods for your dog 59
   What to do if your pet is poisoned 60

9. CHEWING AND MOUTHING 63
   Mouthing 63
   Chewing 65
   Types of Chew 66

10. RECALL TRAINING PREPARATION 68
    Basic Training 71
    Getting to know his name 72

Look at Me	72
Teach him to Sit	73
Teach him to Lie Down	74
Teach him to stay or wait	75
Leash training	75
11. THE FOUNDATIONAL CUES	76
Decide on your cue	77
Sit Stay and Release	78
Other behaviors	80
12. RECALL TRAINING	81
Get him used to coming to you	82
Training sit-stay	83
Sit stay come	83
Going Outside - enclosed area	84
Using the long-line	86
Using a Clicker	89
Recall Summary and where the Clicker fits in	90
Proofing	92
Emergency stop	93
What not to do	94
13. GOING TO THE PARK	97
Other dogs and their communication signals	99
How dogs greet each other	100
How to interact with humans	102
Games	103
14. LEASH AND HEEL TRAINING	105
How to hold the leash	105
Walking to heel	106
Establish the heel position	106
Start walking	108
Meeting other dogs while on the leash	109
Advanced Training	110
15. SEPARATION ANXIETY	112
Not all dogs are the same	113
Causes and Signs Of Separation Anxiety	114
What to watch out for	117

Why Punishment Won't Work	118
Preparation and Socialization	119
How to leave and return	122
Leaving when using a crate	124
Some other useful tips	125
The 10 Steps to help Separation Anxiety	126
16. GROOMING	127
17. FAMOUS GERMAN SHEPHERDS	129
18. CONCLUSION	138
19. LEAVE REVIEW	141
Resources	143

INTRODUCTION

German Shepherds are undoubtedly one of the most famous dog breeds. They have been in the Top 10 of favorite dogs in the US for many years and once you get to know them, it's easy to know why.

Not only are they extremely intelligent, obedient, and loyal but they also have a long and noble history. It is useful to understand this history when it comes to understanding his behavior - and what a great history it is!

Despite his wolf-like appearance, the German Shepherd - also known as GSD - is a relatively modern breed of dog, with its origin dating to the late 1890's in Germany. They were originally working shepherd dogs hence the origin of the breed name. More on this later.

Because of their intelligence and breed background, as well as their high energy (especially when they are puppies), these dogs are best suited to a home that has some knowledge of dogs, rather than a first-time dog parent. They also prefer to focus on one leader and they will need lots of exercise.

I use this term leader deliberately because in the world of German Shepherds 'leader' is used more often than 'parent', and for good reason, but it doesn't mean that this should be confused with dominance.

German Shepherds, like all dogs, respond better to operant reinforcement training than any other type of training method. It is often described as positive reinforcement but there is more to it and the positive quadrant is just one of four.

In the following pages, we will celebrate this wonderful dog describing the key training differences, and the different types of GSD that make up this magnificent breed. And we also honor some of the most famous German Shepherd dogs - this dog must surely have more hero's than any other.

Even although my grand-parents and their parents were German Shepherd lovers and owners, the first German Shepherd that I met as a child was a police dog. I used to change my route home from school on days when I thought I might catch a glimpse of him coming home from his police work. I was fascinated by him.

Much later, I got to know one again but I never met him. He was called Cory and he had run from his family in a remote area. Clearly his family loved him very much, including the two young children who he had protected and looked out for from the very beginning of their lives. I still don't really understand why (I didn't know the family) but I found myself involved in his search over many weeks.

During this process, I had to learn much more about their habits and temperament as well as learning about how to track a lost dog. I also met many owners and parents of German Shepherds, as well as other types of Shepherds, and once again became enthralled with this special dog and his specific beautiful nature, particularly that very first police dog that had captivated me so much.

While there are many things that a German Shepherd has in common with other breeds, if you don't already have or know a German Shepherd, and are thinking of getting one then here are a few things that you need to know :-

1. They are big shedders and tend to do so twice a year usually in the Spring and Fall. If you don't groom them everything in your house will be covered in hair.
2. They will want to be with you all the time and they will follow you everywhere. If you don't want a dog to be more-or-less beside you at all times then a German Shepherd is far from ideal.
3. They are prone to separation anxiety. They might not bark and destroy furniture like most other breeds, but that doesn't mean that they are not stressed by it. Watch out for diarrhea and an unusual amount of shedding. It is, therefore, important that you know someone who can watch him when you are not at home and, if you can't do this, then introduce him to a kennel or daycare at a young age.
4. German Shepherds are not dogs that you can ignore. If you don't want a dog you have to interact with every day then a German Shepherd is not for you.
5. When you take your German Shepherd out for a walk people will either completely adore him or be terrified of him. Some dog owners will walk to the other side of the street or their dog will bark furiously at him and your well-behaved dog will somehow get the blame - as will you. Try, as best you can, to ignore this.

They are smart, loyal, humorous, playful, loving and

beyond all else - devoted to you. They truly are special and wonderful dogs.

As well as covering the history, health and breed types of the German Shepherd I will also cover general puppy training including:-

- How to potty train and house-train your puppy
- Crate Training and the best size of crate
- How to get your puppy to pay attention
- Indoor and enclosed recall training
- Sit, stay, and come
- Walking to heel
- Leash, off-leash and recall
- Proofing
- Emergency stop
- Going to the park
- Causes of Separation Anxiety
- How to prevent Separation Anxiety

The aim of this book is to introduce you to the wonderful German Shepherd Dog and guide you through some early puppy training. Don't forget that GSD's need training, and I would highly recommend taking him or her to training classes.

Finally, choosing the right breeder is more important with GSD's than it can be for other breeds. You must do your homework on who you are buying your puppy from. I outline what expect from an ethical breeder and how to spot one the is not. You will also find some great Facebook groups with lots of GSD owners happy to help as well as local kennel clubs.

1

A BRIEF HISTORY OF GERMAN SHEPHERDS

In Germany, in the 1850's, dogs were bred in villages and they were bred to help the farmers herd their sheep and to protect the sheep from predators. The skills required in order to do this included the ability to be trained (intelligence), speed and strength (they had to be able to travel distance for many hours), as well as a good sense of smell. The German Shepherd became known for having all the these skills.

Herding dogs moved large distances based on the human practice of moving livestock from one grazing ground to another depending on the season, typically to lowlands in winter and highlands in the summer.

As they moved and protected the livestock across the land, these dogs met other dogs to breed with, which introduced new genes to the blood-lines, slowly evolving our herding dogs.

The German Shepherd that we know today can be traced to around 1859, thanks to a genetic study in 2018. From France, he is descended from the Berger Picard, and from Italy he is from the five Italian herding breeds: the Bergamasco Shepherd, Cane Paratore (often disputed as a breed in Italy), Lupino del

Gigante, Pastore d'Oropa, and the Pastore della Lessinia e del Lagorai.

As industrialization got underway, and we moved out of the countryside and into towns and cities there was less need for GSD's (or people) to perform herding work. As towns and cities were built, there was less land available for farming, and both these effects meant that sheepdogs were no longer needed in the same way that they had been in the past.

Luckily, by this stage, our German Shepherd sheepdogs had already established their reputation as a versatile and intelligent breed.

Max Emil Friedrich von Stephanitz

Max Emil Friedrich von Stephanitz, a German dog breeder, is credited with developing the German Shepherd as we know him today, and who first set guidelines for the breed standard.

He was born on Dresden and became a Calvary officer rising to Captain and, during this journey, he studied Veterinary Science in Berlin. He left the Calvary not long after 1898.

Von Stephanitz believed that dogs should be bred for working and he purchased his first GSD, Hektor Linksrhein, at a breeding show in 1899 and changed his name to Horand von Grafrath.

Hektor, or Horand, was himself the product of selective breeding and demonstrated what Von Stephanitz believed a good working dog should be - strong, intelligent, loyal, and beautiful to look at.

Using his training from the Veterinary College in Berlin, he established a 'grand design' that he wanted all breeders to conform to and this included the angle of bones, proportions, and measurements.

After buying Horand, Von Stephanitz founded the Society for German Shepherd dogs and Horand was to be the first dog added to the society's breed register. By 1923, the Society had 50,000 members.

Horand became the primary breeding stud and, along with his sons (Hektor von Schwaben being the most famous), and grandsons (Heinz von Starkenburg, Beowolf and Pilot), they are the foundation of the standardization of the German Shepherd breed. It is from Beowolf that all German Shepherds draw their genetic link.

The German Shepherd is now the second-most registered breed by the American Kennel Club and the seventh-most registered breed by The Kennel Club in the UK. The German Shepherd Society or S.V. (Verein für Deutsche Schäferhunde) is still going strong today.

Because of Max Emil Friedrich von Stephanitz's leadership in creating such a successful Breeding Society he is credited with creating the German Shepherd dog.

The War

During the first half of the twentieth century, the breed came to be strongly identified with Imperial and Nazi Germany.

At the end of World War I, many believed that the inclusion of the word "German" would harm the breed's popularity because of the anti-German sentiment following the war, and the breed was renamed by many international Kennel Clubs, including the UK's, to "Alsatian Wolf Dog".

The second World War and Hitler added to distrust of the name further. Adolf Hitler had a German Shepherd called Prinz and during his years in poverty, he had sent his dog away to be looked after. The dog managed to escape and she found Hitler again who loved her loyalty and her breed as a result. Hitler went on to own several German Shepherds and he was often portrayed as being an animal lover in Nazi propaganda.

German Shepherds were also used widely as guard dogs including the concentration camps during the Holocaust.

The name "wolf dog' was eventually dropped because, according to concerned breeders, the name suggested a wolf-dog hybrid but it was another 50 years before the name Alsatian was allowed to be replaced by German Shepherd by the UK Kennel Club. It was not until 2010 that the parenthesis "Alsatian" was removed altogether.

GSDs became popular in the United States in the early 1900s and were recognized by the AKC in 1908. Their popularity was probably due to the adventures of canine movie stars Rin-Tin-Tin and Strongheart who are featured later in this book as well as guide dog organization founded by GSD's, The Seeing Eye.

The Working Dog

German Shepherds are popular working dogs. They are known for being easy to train, good at performing tasks and excellent at learning and following instructions. They also have a keen sense of smell and can work regardless of distractions.

They are one of the most widely used breeds in a wide variety of scent-work roles including search and rescue, searching for bodies, sniffing out narcotics, explosives, accelerant as well as mine detection.

As a result they are well known for their police and military work as well as search and rescue.

They were used in World War II as messenger dogs, rescue dogs and personal guard dogs. At one time the German Shepherd was the breed chosen almost exclusively to be used as a guide dog for the visually impaired.

Formal guide dog training and the creation of The Seeing Eye (and guide dog schools all around the world) came about because of an article Dorothy Eustis wrote in 1927, titled The

Seeing Eye, about training German Shepherds as guide dogs for World War I veterans.

Dorothy Eustis was an American dog trainer who was, at the time, living in Switzerland where she trained female German Shepherds as Police Dogs.

The article was read by Morris Frank, an American from Tennessee, who became blind in both eyes due to separate accidents in his childhood, and he asked Eustis if she would teach him how to train guide dogs.

In 1928, Eustis invited Frank to Switzerland to train with a German Shepherd guide dog called Kiss. Frank renamed Kiss, Buddy, and all 6 of his dogs that followed were also called Buddy and were GSD's.

Frank returned to the US a few months later and, in 1929 in partnership with Eustis, The Seeing Eye was incorporated in Nashville. It was the first guide-dog school in the United States and was to become the largest. It remains one of the largest to this day and is now based in New Jersey.

Today, most guide dogs are Labradors and Golden Retrievers although there are still German Shepherds being trained.

2

TYPES AND LINES

German Shepherds are medium to large-sized working dogs and are classed within the herding group by the American Kennel Club.

GSD's typically weigh between 70-100lbs, stand 20-24 inches in height and live 9-14 years.

Their strengths across intelligence, trainability, loyalty, and obedience have, over the years, meant that German Shepherds across the world are often the preferred breed for work, including disability assistance, search-and-rescue, police and military roles, and acting and why these dogs have the most hero dogs than almost any other breed.

The 3 key skills are obedience protection and tracking (they would track the location of the sheep and protect them against predators). Because of these skills they are used in protection, rescue, and in the military to name a few areas in which they excel.

German Shepherds are sometimes known by their owners as German Shedders because they shed lots of hair. They have a dense second coat with a thick undercoat and it comes in two variants - long and short. The long-haired type is rarer (and is considered a fault by the American Kennel Club).

They tend to be tan and black or red and black and most have black masks and body markings. Rarer colors include sable, pure black, pure white, liver, silver, blue to name a few.

The sable (silver, grey, and tan hair tipped with black) is considered to be the original DNA while the all-white GSD's get instant disqualification from showing because they are considered to be serious faults.

There are also well-known health issues with GSD's and I will outline the main health problems and reference some recent research into the prevalence of each one.

There are 5 main lines of German Shepherd dogs as well as several varieties. The lines fall broadly into the working line and the show line (I have also added the pet line). The main features of each of these GSD's and the other types such as the King Shepherd variety are described in the following pages.

The Show Line

Show Lines are German Shepherds who have been trained and bred as show dogs and for obedience. Because of this, they can suffer from health problems particularly and the angulation (or slope) of their hindquarters has been under scrutiny over recent years.

Show Line dogs tend to display a lower need for stimulation than their working line cousins. It means that show line dogs can also make good pets.

American and Canadian Show Line

The American Show Line is also called the AKC (and the Canadian is CKC) and this line is typically taller and longer than the other lines. Their coats are solid black, black and tan, saddle sable and solid white. These GSD's have the lightest colors of all the lines and are most likely to have black and tan saddles/coats.

They tend to have less of a working drive and less energy than working lines. Despite this, these GSD's are very active but with low strength. It means they are not great for personal protection or law enforcement but they make great family dogs.

They are bred only for shows and to comply with the rules of the show where there is a focus on movement and appearance (extreme angulation of the hindquarters) and as a result, they have the most angled backs in the hindquarters of all lines.

Additionally, the American breed standards don't emphasize health, unlike the European SV standard. The European Standard emphasizes elbow and hip, intelligence, temperament, and working ability and not movement and appearance meaning that the European dogs ought to display better heath.

Because the American Kennel Club has no requirements for breeding other than that both parents must be registered purebreds of the same breed it can mean, although this breed is generally relaxed with a lower working drive than other lines, there is a risk that the temperaments can be varied due to dogs being bred together where both of the breeding pair have temperament issues.

It means that although this line does make good companions and pets, it is important to research the breeders if you are buying an American or Canadian show line.

West German (European) Show Line

Considered by many to be the most beautiful German Shepherd breed, they are very gracious movers, are very intelligent, and can be easily trained but they need a lot of exercise.

Like their American and Canadian counterparts, they too, are bred for appearance and movement however, their backs are straighter, preventing any excessive sloping to reduce commonly seen issues.

In terms of their coats, they tend to have black and red saddles and can be black and tan, sable, bi-color, and black. Ideally, they should be red with a black saddle.

They have to be fully fit before they can breed, and must pass tests to ensure that their joints and hips are in good condition as well as demonstrating that they are as skilled at working as they are at showing.

The main focus, in terms of working tends to be obedience, intelligence and loyalty all of which means that they should have a better drive and better health than the American Show Line GSD's and with less likelihood of displaying the health problems like hip and elbow dysplasia.

Because of selective breeding, these show-line German Shepherds have less chance of developing issues relating to ill temperaments. Any traits considered unwanted in the dog intended for breeding will not pass the tests and will not be allowed to breed.

The European lines uphold the authenticity of the original breed standards and these strict regulations help produce reliable well-rounded dogs.

Working Line

Working German Shepherds are believed by some of the best specimens of the breed. They are bred for temperament and 'workability'.

They tend to be high on drive and energy and need a strong handler and leader that provides structure and lots of training. Early and good sociability is very important for these working dogs. They do not do well in non-working environments.

With less focus on size and also with less angulation in the lower backs (they have the straightest backs of any of the lines), they have to display both obedience and protection skills. They generally have a large 'square' head, thick paws and thick bone structure.

West (German) Working Line

West Working Line GSD's have a very stable temperament and with long hair they look stunning. They were bred to have a strong working drive and ability, but also a stable temperament both in the working field and away from it.

Their coats come in many colors from black, sable, black and tan, and bi-color. They have a strong drive and excellent working ability and their bodies were bred to have more of a working structure than the West German show lines.

However, their back is more sloped than the East German Working Line and as a result may encounter more health issues.

They excel in a number of jobs including search and rescue or guard and protection and they are eager to please with a cool temperament. They know when to stay calm or when to be aggressive and it makes them good for family life.

East German Working Line DDR

DDR stands for Deutshe Demokratishe Republik and goes back to the time of WWII when the East Germany Government introduced a strict and controlled breeding program for German Shepherds.

This meant that only those dogs who had good health records (free of hip and elbow problems), had a strong working drive and working ability with good athleticism as well as good temperaments were allowed to be bred or registered.

They were primarily used for working with the East German army and police/law enforcement – especially with the military.

These dogs have the darkest coats of all GSD's - usually black or sable and some can be solid black. Their backs are a little slopey and they can resist harsh weather and long working days.

They can also have more of a defensive nature. They still have very strict breeding standards and are only allowed to breed if they are free of hip dysplasia and puppies are tested for proper bone structure before they can be adopted.

Czech Working Line

This is a specialized breed that was, as you might expect, bred in Czechoslovakia. As you might not expect, the breeding was limited to just one kennel and just one purpose. It was started in 1955 at Pohranicni Straze by the Czechoslovakian Army's border patrol and the aim was to singularly breed and train for military border patrol.

They are similar to the East German working lines, but with straighter backs, and they are thought to have a higher work intensity with slightly more agility and protection instincts than their East German cousins. They are very athletic with good stamina and are very intelligent which means they will require a lot of exercise.

While this line has calmed over the years, they are still

work-focused. If you opt for a Czech puppy, you must check the breeder and ensure a proper temperament for your family.

These GSD's coats are longer with darker colouring and their backs are less 'slopey'. They tend to be brown to back or grey and their ears are a little bit smaller than the other 4 breeds with thick chests and paws.

Pet Line

The pet line GSD's come from either home breeding (unregulated) or Show line and Working line generations that have not made the grade. Ideally choose a pup from a breeder because, although they may not have the qualities required to be show line or working line, they will have good genetics overall.

The American Pet Line is most similar to the American Showline with the same appearance.

Variants

East-European Shepherd

The East-European Shepherd (EES) is a variety of the German Shepherd bred in the former Soviet Union.

The East European Shepherd is a large athletic dog, with a long back. He is powerfully built and very intelligent and although muscular, he is not stocky.

His medium-length double-coat is very thick and is usually saddled. The colors tend to be tan and black, red and black, solid black, blue, white or silver, due to a well-developed undercoat. The coat color is typically described as 'saddled' with a blanket of a contrasting color over the shoulders and backline.

He was created around the 1950s by mixing breeds native to

Russia such as the East Siberian Laika, the Caucasian Shepherd, and the Central Asian Shepherd. The aim was to create a larger, more cold-resistant version of the German Shepherd - one that could cope with the sub-zero conditions and that was also a good guard dog.

Because he was originally trained as a guard dog his skills are focused on guarding and protecting which means that he is not ideal as a family pet but with the right training from a strong leader he can be a great companion.

King Shepherd

The King Shepherd is a variety of the German Shepherd introduced in 1990 that is still thought to be in development.

The breeders wanted to have a dog that was similar in nature and appearance to the GSD but less genetic health concerns.

Kings are a mix of German Shepherd with Alaskan Malamute, the Great Pyrenees and sometimes the Akita, and the Swiss Mountain Dog is known to be in the mix too.

Although they are larger than the GSH and look more intimidating they have a good temperament.

GSH's are generally easy-going and approachable within the family and with people they know but they typically don't like strangers and will show aggression to protect their family if they feel threatened.

Although Kings are also protective of their family they are more friendly with anyone as long as they are non-threatening. Their sheer size is intimidating enough.

Kings can often be confused with a long-haired German Shepherd but Kings are larger (there are some shorter tail versions too). Just like all GSD's, they are going to need a lot of grooming - they are big shedders.

The biggest difference is their health. Although the King is still predisposed to some of the conditions that the German Shepherd faces the breeders have worked to remove some of the genetic health problems of GSD's.

Shiloh Shepherd

The Shiloh Shepherd is a variety of the German Shepherd bred in the United States and developed in the 1970s in New York by Tina Barber. Barber wanted a larger, gentler version of the German Shepherd.

Documentation of the crosses used in the breed's development is limited but GSDs were likely crossed with Alaskan Malamutes and German Shepherd dogs with the main foundation of the Shiloh being the German Shepherd.

It has been bred for large size, length of their back, temperament, and soundness of hips to remove some of the health problems of the 'parent' breed although he can still suffer from some of the more common ailments.

Like the GSD he is a very intelligent, courageous, loyal, and self-confident dog that is a good companion that will protect his family and friends.

In general, Shilohs are softer in temperament than GSDs and not used for serious protection work. Shilohs can excel in assistive service, obedience, herding, therapy work, and search and rescue. Bred mainly as companions, Shilohs have loyal and outgoing personalities.

They're typically patient with children and tolerate other animals and they thrive on inclusive activities and companionship.

The Shiloh Shepherd's has a broad back and head. The muzzle should be black and his tail will be relatively long with thick hair that hangs down. His coat will either be smooth or long.

The long coat is medium-length with a dense undercoat and has a distinct mane from the neck to the chest. The smooth coat is thick and medium-length with the outer hair being harsh to touch.

When it comes to training, remember that Shilohs are typically food-driven unlike the more common toy-driven GSD.

Shiloh's were registered as a breed in the 1990s and the International Shiloh Shepherd Registry, Inc. (ISSR) was incorporated in 1991. Today, there are several Shiloh Shepherd registries.

White Shepherd

The White Shepherd is a variety of the German Shepherd bread in the United States although they were originally bred in Germany as far back as the 1880s, they were banned from registration in that country in the 1930s.

By the late 1960s the breed had gained a following in the United States and Canada and a breed club was formed.

They are registered with the United Kennel Club (UKC) in the United States which allows these dogs to be registered under their name of White Shepherd.

White Shepherds have a very good nature and are most often described as cheerful and tranquil and are usually not aggressive.

They are very like German Shepherds in almost every way except for the color of their coats and, like most German Shepherds, they need a lot of exercise. These playful dogs will enjoy playing fetch or frisbee.

They are slightly more prone to separation anxiety and again, like most GSD's, they should be well socialized early on. White Shepherds can also be vocal - trending to whine, moan or grumble.

It is also important to note that many white German shepherds suffer from food allergies, so you may need to talk to your vet about hypoallergenic options.

White Swiss Shepherd

The White Swiss Shepherd Dog, also known as Berger Blanc Suisse, is a descendant of the American White Shepherd that was first registered by the AKC in 1917. It was imported to Switzerland in the 1970s before being recognized as a separate breed in 1991 by the Swiss Kennel Club.

The UK Kennel Club describes this dog as a versatile working, companion dog. Attentive, alert, resilient as well as having a "Lively and friendly temperament, never shy or aggressive. Can be reserved. Easily trained."

Almost all descriptions of this breed comment on his gentle nature. Like GSD's he is very intelligent (and will need good mental exercise), is loyal and faithful, with one general criticism - he can get too attached to his leader and is going to require lots of attention. Separation training is a must.

The White Swiss Shepherd Dog can be slightly wary of strangers, but not aggressive. He won't show trust easily and will only tend to show signs of affection to his owners or people he knows.

Sable German Shepherd

The Sable German Shepherd is not a mixed breed but, as a variant, they carry the same characteristics and temperament of the German Shepherd.

3

HEALTH

German Shepherds are in a group of breeds classed as 'Category Three' by The Kennel Club in the UK, which is the highest category of the health concerns due to their conformation.

This means that these types of dog have been bred over many years to look a certain way, but that these changes to the way they look have started to cause them health problems. For German Shepherds, this is mostly due to the shape of their back legs and hips and this is most prevalent among the showlines.

We go into more detail on some of the health issues below. Here is a summary of the most common conditions:

- **Hip dysplasia** – the hip joint doesn't fit together perfectly caused by a malformation of the ball and socket of the hip joint. It will eventually lead to arthritis. There is a screening test.
- **Elbow dysplasia** – a condition where a dog's elbow socket doesn't form properly, leading to pain and problems. There is a screening test.

- **Canine Degenerative Myelopathy (DM)** – also known as Chronic Degenerative Radiculomyopathy (CDRM) causes weakness to back legs leading to paralysis. There is a screening test.
- **Inherited eye diseases** – including cataracts and multifocal retinal dysplasia. There are screening testing for these.

Common illnesses

VetCompass collects clinical data from vets in the UK. The information described below is from data collected in 2013 on German Shepherds.

It was one of the largest surveys of its type, and provides a useful indicator of common illnesses. The study is one of the largest analysis of demography, mortality and disorder prevalence in GSD's based exclusively on primary-care veterinary clinical records.

Overall, over 63% of GSDs that had presented to veterinarians in the year of the study had at least one disorder recorded during 2013. The most common disorders recorded were ear infections (8%), arthritis/joint disease (6%), diarrhoea (5%), overweight/obesity (5%) and aggression (5%). Male dogs were more likely than female dogs to have aggression (7% versus 3%).

The Top 20 common disorders at a detailed level were as follows:

- Otitis externa
- Osteoarthritis
- Diarrhoea
- Overweight/obesity
- Aggression
- Dental disease
- Ear disorder

- Lameness
- Underweight
- Hip dysplasia
- Skin cyst
- Skin disorder
- Vomiting
- Stiffness
- Anal sac impaction
- Hypersensitivity disorder
- Conjunctivitis
- Laceration
- Atopic dermatitis
- Anal furunculosis
- Cryptorchidism

Hip & Elbow Dysplasia

Dysplasia refers to poorly formed joint anatomy, in this case affecting the hips and/or elbows. This is a genetic condition usually inherited from the parent. Screening of parent dogs is actively encouraged so that only dogs with sound joints are used for breeding.

For pups that inherit badly shaped joints, they will be prone to inflammation which is likely to cause pain when the dog exercises. In the short term, the dog may be lame or limp, or have difficulty such as jumping up.

In the long term, that constant inflammation can lead to joint remodeling and premature arthritis. For some dogs, this can be disabling and impair their enjoyment of life, which is all the more heartbreaking because this can happen to young dogs.

Management of hip or elbow dysplasia means being careful of the puppy's activity levels whilst his bones are still maturing.

It's important to avoid excessive tiredness and over-exercise, since the muscles supporting the joints then become less supportive and joint damage becomes more likely.

In addition, giving a joint supplement can help to protect the joint surfaces.

Dogs with mild dysplasia can often be managed with rest and pain-relieving medications, however, those most seriously affected may need surgery, including specialist replacement joint surgery.

The best way to ensure your dog is less prone to any of these conditions is to buy from a reputable breeder and to ensure you get health clearances from both of the parents.

Gastric Dilatation Volvulus (GDV) or Bloat

German Shepherds are prone to something called Gastric Dilatation Volvulus (GDV). This is when the stomach fills with air and twists on its axis preventing the passage of food and water which can stop the flow of circulation to the stomach and intestines. This can be life-threatening.

It is a serious condition and as soon as this happens you must take your dog to the vet right away. If the stomach is not returned to its natural position then it can be fatal.

To prevent this happening, try not to feed him for at least 45 minutes before exercise and don't feed him until as least 45 minutes after exercise. You can also reduce the chances of bloat by feeding small meals spread throughout the day and by using a bowl designed to make it difficult for your dog to eat too quickly.

Elbow dysplasia

A condition where a dog's elbow socket doesn't form properly, leading to pain and problems. There is a screening test for this.

Canine Degenerative Myelopathy (DM)

Also known as Chronic Degenerative Radiculomyopathy (CDRM) causes weakness to back legs leading to paralysis.

This disease usually appears in dogs from 8 or 9 years of age (Cherubini et al 2008, Rusbridge no date), however, animals as young as 6 months can be affected (Cherubini et al 2008).

Degenerative myelopathy (DM) is a fatal, chronic, progressive, degenerative disease of the spinal cord of several breeds of dog, including the German Shepherd Dog. There is no treatment for this disease and in time it leads to complete paralysis in all limbs.

The first signs of DM involve the hindlimb which will appear to be swaying when moving.

As the disease progresses, hindlimb weakness occurs, leading to an inability to stand and then complete hindlimb paralysis.

If allowed to progress, the disease will spread up the spinal cord to the forelegs leading to tetraplegia (inability to use all four limbs) (Awano et al 2009).

There is currently no effective treatment for this disease or its effects, though physiotherapy can help some dogs stay mobile for longer.

DM is a non-painful disease (Cherubini et al 2008, Shell 2008), however, the dog may be caused distress by its progressive inability to move normally.

DM is considered a common problem in older GSDs but the exact percentage of GSDs affected is currently unknown. Researchers at Missouri University suggest that a relatively high proportion of individuals have the predisposing gene.

In one study 2% of all GSDs presented at USA veterinary teaching hospitals were found to be affected (Coates et al 2007).

In terms of identifying if your dog is at risk of developing the disease, DNA testing can now be undertaken to identify animals at risk of developing the disease and carrier animals, who have a copy of the mutated gene but which are unaffected by the disease themselves.

All dogs should ideally be tested prior to purchase and breeding.

Anal Furunculosis (Perianal Fistulae)

This is a painful disease that causes ulceration around a dog's bottom.

Although anal furunculosis (AF or PF) can affect other breeds (Irish setters, black Labradors and other large breeds), it is most commonly found to affect older German Shepherds.

AF affects the area surrounding the anus resulting in ulceration, inflammation and fistulas.

It is intensely painful for your dog, and straining and crying out when defecating, and persistent licking of the anal area are the most commonly reported clinical signs.

Diagnosis of the condition is usually straightforward.

It has also been suggested that there are similarities between AF and Crohns' disease in humans. It is now widely believed that the disease is a result of a faulty immune system, affecting the gut and the perineum leading to ulceration of the local area.

Additionally, it is now believed by many that anal furunculosis might not be an isolated condition and that dogs often present along with a chronic skin and gut problems, chronic diarrhoea and many have irritable bowel syndrome.

There are common immunosuppressive drug treatments that are sold under brand names. It can work well although the clinical remission obtained with a treatment course can be temporary, with a relapse occurring in more than 60% of dogs when the treatment stops.

This means that continued use of the drug at very low doses may be needed to maintain complete control of the disease.

Some dogs may require anal sac surgery and, in some cases, dietary changes can help.

Natural remedies have also been reported to work (but under less stringent clinical test conditions) and these range from apple cider vinegar, manuka honey and aloe vera.

Eyes

German Shepherd Dogs are predisposed to a type of pink eye (conjunctivitis) called plasma-cell conjunctivitis. This is inflammation of the moist tissues of the eye and it is related to immune-mediated diseases in which the body's immune system attacks its own tissues.

Pannus is an autoimmune disease that is also known as Chronic Superficial Keratitis. It affects the cornea and it can result in blindness if not treated. There are many reasons why GSDs are more predisposed to Pannus and why some are more affected than other dogs.

GSDs and GSD-mixes are more predisposed to Pannus due to their genetic makeup.

Because Pannus is an autoimmune disorder, your GSDs' immune system, is attacking your GSDs' conjunctiva.

UV rays can cause Pannus and so GSDs living at high altitude and near water can develop a more severe case of Pannus because they are more exposed to UV rays.

Air pollutants may be partly responsible for developing Pannus. So, GSDs residing in polluted areas are more susceptible.

Middle-aged GSDs are more affected because of their low immune system.

According to vets, Pannus usually starts at the very edge of the transparent part of the eye known as the cornea. The corner edge of the cornea becomes cloudy with very small, visible blood vessels which will eventually cover the whole cornea. Fortunately, Pannus is not painful.

Here are other visible symptoms of Pannus eye disease in German Shepherds:

- A cloudy pink mass on the cornea and visible blood vessels
- Dark brown or black pigmentation of the cornea
- Inflamed third eyelid
- Eyes watering
- Thick cloudiness of the cornea
- Tiny white spots visible around the eyes

There is no known cure for Pannus but most vets recommend symptomatic treatments which can delay the progress of Pannus and improve their quality of life.

The following are just some examples and you should always take the advice of your veterinary as treatments can change.

Some of the treatments are:

- Dog Protective Sunglasses can reduce UV radiation which can prevent the disease from getting worse.
- Steroid-based Topical Medicine is often recommended by vets to reduce the inflammation. This is usually a corticosteroid eye cream.
- Immunosuppressant Eye Drops might also be prescribed by your vet to improve the scarring and pigmentation of the cornea.
- Some vets may also recommend regular corticosteroid injections together with topical eye treatment. This is more normally recommended for GSD's who are close to blindness

- If a secondary infection has occurred then antibiotics will also be prescribed to prevent the spread of the infection.

Ears

His ears will be one of the things you love most about your GSD. You will really enjoy watching him grow into his ears especially when he is around 3 or 4 months and they stick, oversized, high above his head.

There are a few obvious things that you need to do to look after your GSD's ears - and this is not unusual across breeds. Watch out for ear scratching and try to deal with the cause as soon as you can. If he scratches his ear too much it will bleed and it will be much harder to cure.

If there is a pungent smell emanating from his ears then he is likely to have an infection. Ear infections can be an on-going issue and you really want to get hold of it early to stop on-going issues and to prevent it becoming much worse and harder to deal with.

Coconut oil may be used as a treatment for parasites, but it is recommended to consult with your vet first. Coconut oil has been proven over the years to contain both antimicrobial and antibacterial properties. Apply a small amount of this to your GSD's ear canal and it may help prevent ear mites and yeast infection in German Shepherd ears.

A deductive and preventive approach to German Shepherd ear infection home remedies, you may want to consider feeding your GSD less starchy meats and food. Starch is known to slow down GSD's metabolism, which in turn may affect its inflammatory response. Cut chicken and whole grain foods from your GSD's diet and substitute them with more turkey or beef.

Otitis Externa is one of the most common conditions amongst many dog breeds but is more likely to affect Cocker

Spaniels, Poodles, Bassets and GSD's. You will notice a wax build-up or a smell and probably both.

Otitis is also often one of the illnesses that insurance companies exclude from policies as an on-going condition (mine excluded it from both my dogs). This is probably due to the fact that, once susceptible, it is likely to keep recurring.

Regularly cleaning your GSD's ears can make all the difference to preventing Otitis taking hold but do not over-clean as this can actually make it worse.

4

HOW TO FIND A REPUTABLE BREEDER

The best place to start is with the Kennel Club but whatever you do, you want to ensure that the breeder you select is a registered member of their respective Kennel Club.

If you find a breeder and they offer you a low price then you can be pretty sure they are not reputable.

Reputable - or ethical - breeders invest in good quality dog food, they have good veterinary care, they tend to only breed their females up to twice year and they work to established breeding plans. All of this means that they spend more on the care of the dogs which is why the cost will be higher.

They are interested in the improvement and preservation of the breed and so they will want to know about you too.

You should expect to be asked questions about the puppy's care and you may be asked to sign a contract that deals with health and should include a return to breeder clause that means you will return the puppy if you can no longer care for him or her.

If you are not quizzed about how you will care for your

GSD puppy then it is likely, no matter how high the cost, that you are not dealing with a reputable breeder.

Other things that can help identify a reputable breeder will be if they have extensive knowledge of GSD's, work with a vet, undertake health screening, and if you have been on a wait list this is another good sign.

They should also be able to show genetic screening and the lineage of your puppy (which should be extensive). Many good breeders also show their dogs or are involved in sports or show activities.

How to recognise a puppy farm

When you are buying a puppy, you might not recognise that you're buying from a puppy farm. Many of these types of sellers are experienced and go to extremes to cover up what they really are.

A puppy farm isn't always obvious, so look out for some important signs at each stage of purchasing your puppy.

Advertising

- If you see an advert online, check how many other ads the seller is running. A puppy farm is more than likely to be advertising more than one litter and may also be advertising different breeds. To check, you can google the number in the advert to find out how often it is being used and for what.
- If the advert claims the puppy has been vaccinated and the puppy is under 6 weeks old then this would indicate the advert is from a puppy farm. (Always request written evidence that your puppy and his mother have been vaccinated).

- If your puppy comes with a passport (and has been imported), make sure that your puppy is 12 weeks old. They should be this age to qualify for a passport. If there is no passport then it is more likely your puppy has come from a country with poor legislation around puppy farming.

The Seller

- Always make sure that you see the puppy at his home and where he has been born.
- Make sure the seller does not have other breeds - most breeders specialist in just one breed and should have a depth of knowledge about German Shepherds. A puppy farmer will not have the knowledge so be prepared to ask some questions (you could use some of the information in Chapter 2).
- Make sure that you see the mum and note how the mother reacts to the seller as well as the overall condition of the mum. She should not be wary of the breeder. But also note how she reacts to the puppy. You want to be sure that she is the mother and not another dog that is being presented to you as the mum.
- As noted above, the breeder should be asking you lots of questions to make sure you can look after your new puppy. If they are not interested in you and how you will care for the puppy, then they are unlikely to be interested in the puppy's welfare.
- Puppy farms often prefer to deal with cash and do not offer refunds or have a no returns policy. You

should always seek a puppy contract that lays out the responsibilities and a returns policy.

5

ARRIVING HOME

Now that you have committed to this wonderful animal it is time to take him home and begin his training.

Your GSD needs investment in training, and if you do this, you will get to know one of the most intelligent and caring dogs of any breed. So don't stop with the fundamentals!

Even before you bring your puppy home try and find out what type of food your puppy has been eating up until this point.

You will want to introduce him to the food you want to use slowly, and you will do this by mixing some of his existing food into the new food you have for him.

The reason you do this is that a sudden change in diet will upset his tummy, make him feel uncomfortable and can lead to unexpected accidents that the puppy just won't be in control over. You will also want to know when (and how often) your puppy is used to being fed.

To change his food, start with a small amount of his new food mixed into what he is used to, then slowly increase the amount until all of his food is the food you have chosen.

This is a rule that you will follow throughout his life. Dogs - and their stomachs - don't like a sudden change in their diet, so always introduce a new dog food slowly, no matter how old your dog is.

The next thing you want to try and do is have something that smells like his previous home. If the current owner or breeder doesn't have something you can take home with you, then ask if you can leave some clothing there for a week or so before you bring him home (a sock or an old towel). You will put this in his crate or basket when he gets home.

If you have a garden (and you should have a garden for a GSD), you will need to puppy-proof it. I can promise you, if there are any gaps in a fence or hedge, your puppy will find it.

Use chicken-wire or something similar, plastic if possible as long as you can can securely block access. You will also want to ensure you have a high fence - at least 6 ft for a GSD.

Don't forget that your puppy will want to chew things, so you will need to puppy-proof any electrical wires (move them out of reach if you can) along with house-plants, some of which are poisonous to him.

And don't forget to pick the name of your puppy! You will want to know this as soon as he gets home so you can start training him by using it.

What's in a name?

Your puppy might already have a name, but if you are reading this before you have picked your puppy's name, then there are a few ways to decide on his name that can make training easier.

For example, the best names end with a vowel sound. This is because dogs hear at a higher frequency range than we do, and so this grabs the attention better. Ideally his (or her) name should start with a hard letter sound like B or D and it should contain two syllables.

You want to avoid any names that your puppy might confuse with one of your cue's or commands (like sit, stay, here or come).

To get him used to his name say it and reward him when you say it even when there is no response. Then, as soon as there is a response, immediately reward with a tastier treat. Just walk around the house and say his name and reward his response.

He's home!

When your pup comes home, you will already have his crate or basket ready. You will have the same type of dog food that he was being fed, and you will have the scented item placed in his crate or his basket so that it smells like his previous home.

Over the first few nights, he is likely to miss his old family. It is okay over these first nights to take his crate or basket into your room but, ideally, only do this for the first few nights.

He also won't be used to lots of noise and activity around him. Try and keep things as calm as possible and make sure to create some 'time-outs' for him.

You can introduce him to his crate by placing it in the room with you.

Don't forget that puppies sleep a lot. They also need their sleep, so try and let them have their sleep time even although everyone will want to play with your new puppy and pick them up and cuddle them. This is okay, and it is actually great for the puppy to have lots of affection and integrate into the entire life of his new family, so just be aware of it.

The best way to pick up your puppy is to put your hands between his front legs and around his chest. Then pull him towards your chest and, at about the same time, and when he is safely secured, take one of your hands and use it to support his bottom so that you are supporting his weight.

As mentioned earlier, puppies sleep a lot. They will easily sleep for 7-8 hours at night, and they will generally sleep up to 14 hours a day. I will talk about a schedule later, and it will include sleep time for him.

Socialization

In its simplest form, socialization is how you and your puppy learn to communicate with each other and how your puppy learns about others he lives with and meets. This includes other humans and other dogs.

Your puppy's first few weeks are really important for his socialization training, but this isn't easy in the first week or two because your puppy has yet to be vaccinated. However, you can still carry him, take him out in your car, and have others come to the house to meet him.

This is also the best time to touch their ears, mouth, tails, and paws and to get him used to you doing this. This part of training is often missed, but it will really help later with grooming or if you need to inspect him for any injury.

Sit with him quietly so that you are also teaching him how to relax with you and touch his ears or mouth, run your hand over his paws and his tail, and give him a treat and reward him when he remains calm and relaxed.

If you can, and as soon as you are allowed, take your puppy to socialization classes where he can meet other young puppies and their parents.

They will play around for 20 or 30 minutes, but they learn how to communicate with other dogs and how 'far they can go.'

They also learn about meeting other humans who are not the family.

Socialization is a very important part of his early training and helps him feel comfortable with other dogs and other people throughout his life. It is particularly important for GSD's who can tend to suffer from separation anxiety too.

Vaccinations over the first year

It's a good idea to talk to your vet about your puppy's vaccination requirements as soon as you can. Below is a summary of the recommended vaccinations from the American Kennel Club, and there are also optional vaccinations that you can give your puppy.

I have only highlighted the recommended vaccinations here.

- 6-8 weeks - Distemper, parvovirus
- 10-12 weeks - DHPP (for distemper, adenovirus (hepatitis), parainfluenza, parvovirus
- 16-18 weeks DHPP, rabies
- 12-16 months DHPP, rabies

Unvaccinated puppies less than 4 months old are most at risk of Parvovirus. Parvovirus is contagious and affects all dogs. There is no cure, and the puppy will need to be kept hydrated and an effort made to control the secondary symptoms.

The Kennel Club recommends talking to your veterinarian about Heartworm treatment when your puppy is 12-16 weeks old. This is a preventative medication that is taken regularly.

These are the sort of issues where any recommendation must come from a qualified pet health professional who understands the laws and problems in your area and who will be aware of any breed-specific problems. Make sure that you ask your veterinarian for advice.

Your puppy can go outside for a walk in the park after his third set of vaccinations (around weeks 16-18). It is also at this point that he can exercise for up to 20 minutes at a time.

He can also now meet unfamiliar dogs. Before this, you can take him to your yard around 7 days after his first set of vaccinations but avoiding other dogs. Your yard must be enclosed to ensure no other dogs have been there. His feet must also not touch the ground in public spaces.

If you live in an apartment, you might need to do this during potty training and to let your puppy relieve himself outside. Pick one spot and carry him there and back, but you can let him sniff around that spot.

After his second vaccination, you can take him for a walk on paved surfaces but not on grass or places where you can't see if other dogs have urinated or gone to the toilet, although I would also suggest that you carry him rather than walk on any surface.

It is still important for them not to meet unfamiliar dogs. It is at this stage, at around 18 weeks, that you can take him to his puppy socialization classes at the local pet store or your vet (where all the other puppies will be at the same vaccination stage).

6

HOUSE AND POTTY TRAINING

House training or potty training your puppy will be one of the first things you do when your puppy comes home.

The speed at which your puppy learns will vary and can also depend on where he came from or if any training has already been started in his previous home.

Even a young puppy's rate of being house trained will depend on what they were taught once they were weaned and walking confidently on their 4 legs. It really is worthwhile getting to know your breeder if you can and getting involved before your GSD comes home.

When we were looking after the puppies we used puppy pads to train them as soon as the were weaned. This meant that when they went to their forever homes, they were easy to train and it was much easier to complete the house training.

They were also used to used to being in a cage. We kept it in the room with them so that they could wander in to play and sleep (and get used to its sound). These small things can really help.

How long can a puppy wait for the toilet

A puppy's bladder grows with them. When they are younger, it is smaller, which means that they will need to empty it more often.

Generally speaking, a puppy's ability to hold his bladder increases by about an hour per month.

This will mean that at one month, they can hold on for about an hour. By 2 months old, they should be able to hold on for about 2 hours before they need to relieve themselves.

Try not to make them hold on for much more than this over the first few months, or there will be accidents, and try to make sure that your time away from them can tie into their need to go toilet.

As a general rule, puppies under 6 months will struggle to hold their bladder for more than 3 or 4 hours, and this should help you work out how long you can be away or when you might need to try and get someone to visit your puppy.

In terms of pooping, a puppy will poop after food. If you feed your puppy before you leave, make sure that you feed them around 45 minutes before you are due to leave.

This gives you time to take them for a poop. They will normally need to poop between 5 and 30 minutes after a meal.

If you are playing with your puppy before you leave, take them out for a poop after the playtime, as this can also make them want to poop.

Puppy Pads

The best thing I have done is use puppy pads and the very best thing I have ever tried was a puppy pad that looked like grass.

Whether you use a fabric pad or a fake grass one, these are the things you need to do.

Start by placing the puppy pad in the room where your puppy will spend most of his time. As soon as he looks like he is about to potty, place him on the pad. If he relieves himself, give him lots of praise.

It won't take long before he starts going to the pad and can be as little as 1-2 days.

Then start to move the puppy pad towards the door that you will use to take him out. Try not to move it too far from where you started the training; just move it slowly to the door. Always try to use the same door as the exit to where he goes to relive himself.

Once at the door, get him used to that for a day or two then move the pad just outside the door.

In the final stages, if you see him starting to relieve himself indoors and not on a pad, then gently pick him up and place him on the pad and take him and the pad outside. If there isn't enough time to do this, just place him on the pad.

You might want to consider placing the puppy pad at the door he will be using to access his outside area right away. This will depend on how far from the room the household congregates in is from that door.

At every point, give your puppy lots of praise.

As long as you remember that he will want to relieve himself when he wakes up, after play, or after he eats, you have a head-start knowing when to expect activity.

It's important never to punish or get angry with your puppy if he toilets in the house. You sometimes see a recommendation to push their face into the mess. Don't do this. It will do the opposite of helping.

They won't understand and will be scared. Getting angry or punishing them may only mean that they don't want to relieve themselves in front of you and learn to avoid this.

How to manage their potty training

Puppy's (and later dogs) love praise and rewards.

Once your puppy begins the process of going outside to relive themselves, don't forget that you need to praise him and give him a treat every single time at the start.

Remember to wait until he has finished so that you don't distract him in the act.

As you do this, use a phrase that he will start to recognize (try not to use 'Good boy' or 'Good girl' - it might cause confusion!). Use a short phrase that you feel comfortable saying and will remember—just make sure it is one that your puppy can begin to recognize with the action he is being asked to complete.

Where?

Choose a place or a small area outside where you want him to relieve himself. As he relieves himself, say your word or a specific phrase.

Always take him to the same place every time you take him out to potty - in the morning, the last thing at night, after food, or after play during the day.

If you are using training pads overnight, take the soiled pad to the area where you want your puppy to toilet. The scent can help him.

When it is time to take him outside to toilet, avoid playing with your puppy and getting him excited before he relieves himself. Remember, they are easily distracted and will forget what they are there to do.

If your puppy looks a bit confused or doesn't toilet right away, just try to encourage him to sniff the ground beside the area you want him to use.

Stay outside with him until he has toileted. If nothing happens after 5 minutes, take him back inside but watch him closely.

After 10 minutes, take him out again and repeat the process until he has done what you need him to do.

Supervise and be vigilant

Try and supervise your puppy all of the time when you are trying to potty train him. I know this is very hard to do as they tend to have a mind and vision of their own.

By supervising and watching them, you will notice not only how they look when they start to feel uncomfortable because they need to toilet, but you will notice how they do it.

For example, they might start circling or sniffing the floor, they might be restless, and they may try and go to a place they have previously done their business.

If you see your puppy mid-toilet, then pick him up and take him outside and try to get him to finish what he started there; if he does, then gently praise him.

Your puppy won't be able to hold his bladder all night long for several months. This means it is likely that he will need to go during the night.

Put some newspaper or puppy pads in his crate but try and place them in an area that he can avoid. In the morning, don't forget to take the soiled pad or newspaper to his garden area.

If you are going out for any length of time, then do the same thing but try, if you can, to be no more than 3 hours at the start.

It may take several months before your puppy is fully house trained, but the accidents will become less frequent. Try and be patient. It will pay off in time.

How to clean up the mess

It's important to clean the area and try to remove the scent.

Don't use ammonia-based products as this will just encourage them to go to the same place again. I have found that cold water can work too - and it is very good at removing any staining. You can use biological powder, and some people swear by a vinegar-water mix.

Create a Schedule

One of the best and most effective ways to train your puppy is to get him used to a schedule.

The key aspects of your schedule will be feeding times, sleeping time (puppies like to sleep a lot), and of course, potty time.

You need to get your puppy into a regular schedule. The quicker you can do this and get him used to this schedule, the easier everything becomes.

Feeding them to the same schedule also means that they will want to relieve themselves in reaction to that schedule. This, in itself, will make it easier for you to house-train.

Your schedule

When you first bring your puppy home, make sure that you take them out frequently. Take them out as soon as they wake up, after playing, and after they have eaten or had a drink.

A useful summary of what you need to do is detailed in these 5 steps:-

1. Feed them at the same time
2. Feed them with the same frequency, for example, every 2 hours depending on their age

3. Take them out them out as soon as they wake up
4. Take them out before they go to bed
5. Take them out after food and after play.

In terms of how a day might look, try not to forget his sleep time. Your puppy will get sleepy after eating.

Just make sure that you take him out to potty right after he has eaten but before he goes for his first morning nap.

Sleep

As mentioned earlier, puppies sleep a lot. When he is young and up to 3 months old, he can sleep up to 18 hours a day, sometimes up to 20!

He can fall asleep suddenly, and it can even appear as if he has fallen asleep mid-step. He will fall asleep with a chew in his mouth or just sit down in the middle of the floor and collapse. When he does, just pick him up and put him in his cage or basket (with the door open).

He should easily sleep for 7 hours at night, and most puppies can sleep for 7 hours without requiring a bathroom break.

Puppies need their sleep, so make sure you don't forget to let him get it. This will be harder than you think in the first few weeks. There will be many visitors and lots of people who will want to pick him up and cuddle him. This is okay but don't forget to give him his sleep time. He needs it.

BUILD this into your schedule so that it might look like this:

7 AM - WAKE up and go outside
    7:30 am - breakfast

7:45 am - playtime
8:00 am - outside for toilet
8:15 am - sleep (with toy in the cage/depart for work?)
10:15 am - outside for toilet
10:30 - food
10:40 - outside for toiler
10:50 - playtime
11:10 - outside for toilet
11:15 am - sleep with Kong or Toy in the cage
1:15pm - wake up/ outside for toilet
1:20pm - food
1:25 - outside for toilet/playtime
1:30 - playtime
2:00 pm - outside for toilet
2:15 - sleep (cage with toy)

You will find a schedule that works for you as you discover when your pup likes to go potty during the day. It might be after food or after playtime. But always take him out as soon as he awakens.

These timings will change as he gets a bit older and sleeps less—but he will always sleep a great deal, up to 14 hours a day.

Bedtime

You will find that your puppy will start to go to bed by himself. He will get used to your schedule and will fit into when you go to bed at night.

In the early days, if they do wake up during the night, don't be tempted to play with them. They will be more than happy to play, but they need to know that this is not the right time. Don't turn on all the lights either. Take them outside to let them toilet and then return them to bed.

By now you will have placed his crate or basket into the room you want him to use. If you are using a crate or basket you might start to move it there at nighttime once he is going in and out of his crate. And recognising his basket as 'his' place.

7
CRATE TRAINING

Many people worry that using a crate might be cruel. If used properly, a crate is a place that your puppy will feel safe and happy. This is the main objective of your crate training.

It brings a range of other benefits that will mean your life with your puppy can be as full and engaging as possible - and allow him to be included in almost all of your activities and even holidays.

The most important use of a crate is to provide a safe place for your puppy. Never use the crate as punishment.

Crate training is also a great way to help house training because dogs don't like to mess where they sleep.

This means that they will do their very best to hold on until they can leave the crate which puts you in more control. You will know where your puppy is and what he might want to do when you open the crate door.

This means as soon as your puppy leaves his crate you need to take him outside. He will soon get used to this routine.

Crate training has lots of other benefits. Your dog will be able to travel with you more easily, in the car or on a plane. You can visit friends and family more easily because you can use the crate as their portable den.

You can go out knowing that you won't return to chewed furniture or a general mess (the chewing usually only occurs with puppies), and your dog can use the crate as his bed and sleep there overnight.

In summary, the crate gives your dog and puppy somewhere safe to rest and to sleep. It helps them feel comfortable when you leave the house; they can feel safe in a new house or room that you both are visiting, and it means that your dog can enjoy more of your life outside of the home if you need to travel.

Introducing your pup to the crate

After picking your crate and before the puppy arrives, add a blanket or something soft for your puppy to lie on.

If you are using a second-hand crate, make sure you wash it thoroughly to remove any scent of the previous dog who may have been using it.

If you are using a wire crate, have something close that you can place on the top or the side of the crate. This can help to make it feel more like a den, especially at night. Don't cover up all four sides, and make sure the front of the crate (where the door is) is left uncovered.

Initially you can place the crate in a room that is used by the rest of the household. This will help the puppy get used to the crate without being separated from you and your puppy's new family, and it will mean he doesn't feel alone and scared. Put his toys and the item from his previous home into the crate.

If you want you can put the crate into the room that you want him to use and follow the steps below. Once you pick your room make sure that you also spend lots of time there with him.

The first stage is to place some food around the crate. If he doesn't start moving towards the crate or being curious about it all by himself, then entice him by calling him to the crate or by throwing tasty treats around and near the crate. Keep trying until he starts to come over to the crate and begins to feel comfortable around it.

The next stage is to slowly start moving the treats to the door and then inside the crate. Give him lots of praise at all stages. Only start moving the food inside the crate once he has started getting used to the outside of the crate. As he starts to enter the crate, don't close the door.

Let him enter and leave and explore the crate if he wants to. You want to get him used to entering and leaving by himself. But keep pushing the treats further into the crate as his confidence grows.

This can take anything from 10 minutes to a few days, depending on his experience to date, to get him to go into his crate by himself. Keep the training sessions to between 3 and 5 minutes.

If your puppy is not responding to food and treats for any reason, then entice him with his favorite toy.

The next phase is to increase the length of time he spends in his crate. You can do this by feeding him in his crate, or you can put a Kong toy filled with treats into the cage for him to play with.

If he is reluctant to go into the crate, put his food bowl beside the crate door and then slowly move it into the crate until he eats at the back of the crate.

Once he is happy entering and leaving and maybe lingering for a few minutes in his crate, try to close the door. You can do this when he is eating, but one of the most effective ways is to give him his Kong stuffed with something he loves.

Wait until he starts to become engrossed in getting his food out of the Kong, then slowly close the door. If you close the door and he gets anxious or scared, immediately open the door.

If he does nothing, then wait for a few minutes before opening the door again.

Keep increasing the length of time before you open the door— you want to try and reach 10 minutes. If he shows any signs of distress, if he is panting, whining, cowering, or showing any signs of aggression, then you will know you have increased the time too quickly.

Once your puppy is happy to stay in the crate up to 10 minutes after eating or playing, then you will know that he is now likely to understand that his crate is a safe space.

The next phase of his crate training can now begin, and this is when you move out of sight while he is in his crate with the door closed.

This is the stage when his toys and his Kong (filled with food, peanut butter, or soft cheese) will really help.

Put his toys in his cage and close the door once he has entered. Stay beside the crate for around 5 minutes before moving quietly from the room and out of sight.

Once you are out of sight, turn around and come back to the side of the crate and sit beside it for 5 minutes. Gradually start to stay out of sight longer.

Do this throughout the day but at different times. You will need to repeat the process several times. It is during this stage, if you haven't already done so, that you will want to move the crate into the room that you want him to use.

If you hear any barking or whining, do not come back mid bark or mid whine. Try and find a gap, and this is when you return. You are aiming to increase the time you are out of sight to around 30 minutes.

Once this has been achieved, you can start leaving the house altogether. But remember to provide toys for him to play with so that he does not get bored. Before leaving, make sure he has had a small meal and has been exercised, and remember to leave calmly without any fuss.

Size of Crate

Unlike the crate's material, the size of the crate you choose is important (although I would not recommend a fabric style crate for a GSD).

If the crate is too small, it will make your dog uncomfortable, and it is too big, it can make your dog insecure. You need to know the height, width, and length of the crate (or kennel).

The easiest thing to do is get an idea of how big your puppy will grow to be. If you are training an older dog (or a dog over 12 months old), measure from the top of his nose to the base of his tail. It's also a good idea to measure the height of your dog when he is sitting down.

To estimate the crate size, you will need to add around 4 inches to your measurement for height and around 2 inches for the length. The width is less important as it will relate to the height.

The next thing you need to do is check your dog's weight or, in terms of your puppy, check the average weight of his breed when fully grown. Then make sure to check the weight limits on the crate you are buying (or you may be able to pick it up from another dog owner who is no longer using their crate).

Finally, to save you from buying different crates as your puppy grows, you can section off a part of the crate with a separator to make it smaller when he is smaller.

Dog Breed Sizing, Height and Weights

Below are the general crate sizes for a GSD. Check with your breeder or veterinarian on your dog's likely final height and weight (some dogs can be smaller or larger than the averages noted below).

LARGE DOG BREEDS 42″ Dog Crate

Dogs weighing between 71-90 lbs and about 23″ - 26″ in height.

Examples only: Australian Shepherd, Boxer, Dalmatian, English Setter, German Shepherd, Golden Retriever, Irish Setter, Labrador Retriever, Rhodesian Ridgeback, Poodle (Standard)

EXTRA LARGE DOG BREEDS 48″ Dog Crate

Dogs weighing between 91 - 110 lbs and ranging from around 26″ - 28″ in height

Examples only: German Shepherd, Afghan Hound, Akita, Alaskan Malamute, Bernese Mountain Dog, Bloodhound, Doberman Pinscher, Giant Schnauzer, Greyhound

8
FOOD AND FEEDING

Diet and Weight

You will change the diet of your GSD over his life. When he is a puppy your aim is weight gain but this is definitely not the aim once he is fully grown.

While German Shepherds have common foods that they should not eat along with most dogs there are some foods that you really want to avoid with your GSD. These include Avocado, Macadamia nuts, ice cream, garlic, cinnamon, chocolate, almonds, onions, grapes, raisins, cherries and mushrooms.

What to feed him

Dogs are built to be meat-eaters, but they are descended from omnivores, so they can survive adequately without meat (if the protein balance is right).

Unfortunately, the protein in meat is not the same as the protein found in plant-based foods, and this is one of the reasons to be careful of the food you give your puppy and your dog.

This doesn't mean that dogs can't live on a plant-based diet; it just means it will need to be supplement with the essential proteins he will require and Vitamin D.

Balancing nutrition is the most important aspect of your dogs' food. For example, we need our carbs for energy, but dogs don't need many carbs.

Dogs and especially puppies need fats and fatty acids. Most of these are contained in animal fats, but some seed and plant oils can provide a concentrated source of energy. You are looking for an Omega-3 family of essential fatty acids.

When looking for dog food, look at the type of calories rather than the overall total. For example, you don't want too much carbohydrates.

Today's average dog food can contain anywhere between 30% and 70% carbohydrates, but in the wild, dogs will intake only about 15%.

An adult dog's diet can contain up to 50% carbohydrate (by weight), up to 4.5% fiber, and a minimum of around 5.5% should come from fats and 10% from protein.

You can read more about nutrition at nap.edu, and this is listed in the resources at the end of this book.

In general, though, if you want to check out how much meat is in your dog food, look at the ingredients list. The further down the meat appears, the lower the meat content.

The most common ingredients today are whole grain, fat, soya, and corn. So if you see chicken by-products, this doesn't mean it is chicken meat. It most likely isn't.

The top ingredients to look for (and look for a range of these in the same food) include deboned chicken or turkey, Atlantic mackerel and herring, chicken and turkey liver, chicken and turkey heart, and other items such as egg and other types of fish. All high in protein.

There has also been some debate about dry food versus wet food. The main difference being that wet food contains more water (around 75%) whereas dry food can contain only about 10% water.

Dry food tends to be more calorie-dense, and wet food has less grain and fewer carbs. Grain isn't necessarily a bad thing; it just depends on quantity.

Dry food lasts for longer and tends to be more cost-effective than wet food.

There are lots of choices on the market, and you will want to research this yourself.

How much to feed

Puppies can require up to double the energy intake of adult dogs. This is based on weight - it doesn't mean they eat twice as much as an adult dog, just that per pound of weight they do - and they weigh a lot less when they are puppies.

GSD puppies can eat too much at this stage, and this might lead to bone or joint problems later. This means it is best to control their feeding and not leave food in their bowl for them to nibble on between meals.

The frequency really does depend on how old they are. A puppy's tummy is small when he arrives home and will grow over time. The means you need to feed smaller amounts more regularly.

Puppies aged 8-16 weeks need to be fed 4 meals a day, perhaps every 3 hours. Pups ages 3 to 6 months should be fed 3 times a day (every 4 hours) and then after that twice a day, in the morning and early evening.

Your aim is to spread their nutrition throughout the day, so space out the times to equal intervals across the day and remember not to feed your puppy just before or after their walk (or playtime).

The amount that you feed your puppy will depend on their

weight and age. The dog food you choose will also have a variety of different protein levels.

When you decide on your dog food, the packaging will tell you how much to feed your puppy, depending on their weight. If you are in any doubt, ask your veterinarian.

What not to feed - dangerous foods for your dog

ALCOHOL - under no circumstances give your dog alcohol. In the worst-case scenario, alcohol can cause death.

CAFFEINE AND CHOCOLATE—don't give your puppy anything with caffeine. Things that can include caffeine are obviously coffee, but chocolate can also contain caffeine. Chocolate, especially dark chocolate, should never be given to your dog. The toxic substances can cause vomiting, irregular heart function, and even death.

If your dog has eaten a lot of chocolate, contact your veterinarian and immediately try to encourage your dog to vomit.

COCONUT (including coconut oil) - in small quantities, might cause stomach upsets, but coconut water should not be given to your dog.

HOPS are used in the process of brewing beer. If you are a home-brew enthusiast, then you must keep hops out of the reach of your German Shepherd. Signs to look out for are increased breathing, a racing heart rate, and vomiting. In severe cases, death can occur.

ONION, CHIVES, AND GARLIC can irritate the bowel and are toxic to dogs.

NUTS (Pecans, Almonds, Walnuts, Macadamia) - these have the potential to not only cause vomiting but possible pancreatitis. Peanuts and popcorn are okay.

RAISINS AND GRAPES - avoid giving your dog raisins or grapes. The effect the toxins have is still not definitive, but it can cause Kidney failure.

This also includes other dried variants like sultanas and currants and any foods containing grape, such as grape juice, raisin cereal, raisin bread, granola, trail mix, and raisin cookies or bars. Early signs are vomiting, diarrhea, and lethargy.

RAW POTATO (or green potato) is poisonous to dogs. It contains a toxic compound called solanine (which is also contained in GREEN TOMATO'S), and if your dog eats a large amount, it will affect his nervous system. Symptoms to look for are blurred vision, vomiting, diarrhea, low temperature, and slow heart rate.

TURKEY AND CHICKEN BONES. Generally speaking, be careful of any bones that you give your dog to chew. If they can easily break them apart, they can lodge in their throats or their intestines. Even lamb joint bones can be dangerous for dogs who can chew through them, and they can be quite brittle. Sharp bones can also puncture their digestive tract.

SHELLFISH - some dogs are ok with shellfish, but one of my dogs will vomit immediately, and this will happen with even small traces of shellfish such as prawns or langoustine. This doesn't mean dogs can't eat fish. They can eat fish, and fish is good for them in many cases. Always ensure it is cooked and sufficiently cooled.

XYLITOL (sweetener) and all foods containing Xylitol is toxic to dogs. It can cause your dog's blood sugar to drop and cause acute liver failure and even death. Early symptoms include vomiting, lethargy, and coordination problems or seizures.

Xylitol is used as a sweetener in several products including candy, gum, baked goods, diet foods, and even some peanut butter and toothpaste.

What to do if your pet is poisoned

These are the instructions from the Pet Poison Helpline:-

- Remove your pet from the area.
- Check to make sure your pet is safe: breathing and acting normally.
- Do NOT give any home antidotes.
- Do NOT induce vomiting without consulting a vet or Pet Poison Helpline.
- Call Your Vet or, in the US, the Pet Poison Helpline at 855-764-7661.
- If veterinary attention is necessary, contact your veterinarian or emergency veterinary clinic immediately.

The detailed instructions from the Per Poison Helpline is as follows:

1. Immediately remove your pet from the area, and make sure no other pets (or kids!) are exposed to this area. Safely remove any remaining poisonous material from their reach.
2. Check to make sure your pet is breathing normally and acting fine otherwise.
3. Collect a sample of the material, along with the packaging, vial, or container, and save it – you will need all that information when you talk to your veterinarian.
4. Do NOT give your dog any milk, food, salt, oil, or any other home remedies! Also, never inducing vomiting without talking to your veterinarian – it could be detrimental
5. Don't give hydrogen peroxide to your pet without checking with a vet or with Pet Poison Helpline first.
6. Get help. Program your veterinarian phone number, along with an ER vet and Pet Poison Helpline's

phone number in your cell phone so you will always have immediate access to help.

Keep in mind that the prognosis is always better when a toxicity is reported immediately, so don't wait to see if your pet becomes symptomatic before calling for help.

Remember that there's a narrow window of time when vomiting can be induced or the stomach pumped in the case of a poisoning.

9

CHEWING AND MOUTHING

Puppies not only chew but there is a period when they will use their mouths - a lot! . This is called mouthing, and their tiny teeth are remarkably sharp. German Shepherds are known to be a mouthy breed - probably because of the herding heritage and so training him not to chew your hand or furniture is essential with this breed.

Puppies need to learn about different textures - and human skin is just one of the textures they need to learn about. They also need to understand how hard they can close their mouths and when enough is enough. They can only learn this by doing it.

Mouthing

All puppies will go through this phase, and you will want to teach them what some people call bite inhibition.

This is something that puppies, who have come from a larger litter, will have learned a bit about because they usually learn this through play with other puppies (and something early socialization classes can help with too).

This is just a part-and-parcel of a puppy growing up and learning boundaries. Puppies are most likely to try and mouth you when you are playing with them, tickling their tummy, or petting them.

First of all - it's important to let your puppy mouth you.

Let him have your hand. When he closes his mouth too hard, and his sharp teeth become painful, squeal like a puppy or use the word "stop" and then stop playing with him. Just let your hand go limp so that it is no fun to play with.

This should stop your puppy for a moment or two. He will be just as surprised as you. When he relaxes his mouth and stops, then praise him. Then let him have your hand again.

He will go too far quite a few times as he learns, so just keep repeating over a 15- or 20-minute time interval until he learns how hard he can close his mouth without hurting you.

If your squealing and "stop' doesn't work, then put him on the "naughty step' so to speak. Stop playing with him for 30 seconds or so. After this, start playing with him again.

If he does it again, then repeat, and if this still doesn't work, then move away from him as soon as he mouths you and you feel that nip.

Eventually, he will know exactly the level of pressure that he can safely apply when he is playing.

Remember not to jerk your hands away from your puppy when he starts mouthing you. He still thinks this is a game and is more likely to lunge forward and don't wave your hands in front of his face for the same reason—he will think it's a game.

Whatever you do, don't hit your puppy for mouthing. This will only make him play harder, but it may also cause him to fear you.

Once you have done this, you want him to learn not to mouth at all on human skin and to let you pet them without being mouthed.

When your puppy tries to mouth you when you are petting them, distract him by giving him a treat or a chew toy.

One last thing to bear in mind. Like all toddlers, puppies can have tantrums. His body will be stiffer, and his mouth might be tighter around the lips.

If you notice this while you are playing with him, just stop the play.

Don't squeal if he bites you (it will be harder than normal). If you are holding him, stop playing but continue to hold him for a few seconds, then let him go.

Don't make him afraid of you—you just want him to know that he has gone too far. If you notice that your puppy continues to have tantrums, you will need to get more help from a professional.

Chewing

All puppies enjoy and need to chew. They do this to explore their environment and understand the texture of things; they don't have hands, and they like to pick things up. So the only way he can explore is to use his mouth.

Between the ages of around three and seven months, your puppy will also start to experience discomfort in his mouth as the teething process gets underway. He will chew to help remove his baby teeth, and he will chew to help with the pain of his adult teeth erupting in his gums.

As your puppy starts to reach adolescence, at around seven to 12 months, his chewing is going to get worse. There are two possible reasons for this.

It is around now that they tend to get easily bored so try to find new games (especially mental exercise games) and other games to keep them occupied.

It is also around this time that their adult teeth are settling into the jaw, which can be uncomfortable for some dogs.

Whatever the reason and it might be both of the above reasons, your puppy is going to chew at things.

You will need to teach everyone in your household to put their shoes out of reach and preferably out of sight along with any toys that have different textures. These will be the favored chew items.

Puppies love shoes—they are just about the right consistency of hard and soft making them perfect for exploring different textures. Much the same as furniture too.

Try and change your dog's chew toys regularly by rotating them every few days. This will prevent him from getting bored and prevent him from looking for something else to chew that might look more interesting.

Try and remove anything you don't want him to chew and keep everything well out of reach. I lost a TV remote control and a pair of glasses by forgetting to move them to higher ground.

Also, don't forget to remove anything dangerous to your puppy when he cannot be supervised. This includes some types of household plants that are poisonous to dogs.

If you find your puppy chewing on something that is not allowed, don't punish him or shout at him. This will only make him anxious. Instead, simply distract his attention and then direct him to a chew toy that you want him to play with. When he starts to play with it, make a fuss of him.

Types of Chew

Many hard plastic toys are not made for chewing by a dog. The best chew toys are made of the type of hard rubber that you get with your Kong.

You can also consider activity balls (like Kong's, you can place kibble, cheese spread, peanut butter, or other treats or food inside). Ropes are also good but avoid nylon or anything that the dog can pull apart into a string.

Chews such as dental chews or other edible chews can distract your puppy—they can be eaten quite quickly. These chews will probably last just a few minutes with your GSD, so you will want to find a chew alternative. It is just a case of testing which chews your puppy likes the most.

10

RECALL TRAINING PREPARATION

Due to their intelligence German Shepherd Dogs are relatively easy to train. You will need a few tools and some equipment to progress with all the training. Here are the main items you will be using:-

TREATS

Treats are the mainstay of dog training at the puppy stage but try and introduce other rewards such as toys or praise too. In a few cases dogs can prefer toys to treats!

Some people cut up hot dogs, I made something called liver cake (it worked really well), and one of the simplest things to do is to grab a handful of his kibble and you this as a dog training treat.

Kibble isn't always seen by your dog as being of high value so work out what his preferred treats are and which ones he loves most.

You will then use this knowledge to reward based on difficulty, the more difficult the higher the reward value. It is important to use more than one treat, try and have a selection of 3 or 4 if you can.

This allows you to always be able to reward on value and, depending on what you want him to do, and how much he might not immediately understand or want to do it, you can use the treat that matches his effort.

For example, if he absolutely loves cheese then save this as a special treat, if he has learned to sit then offer him kibble when he sits.

If he is doing recall and takes a long time to return then he gets kibble, if he returns quickly, he gets the cheese. This process can increase the connection between you and your puppy.

There are a few reasons that treats might not work. They might not be tasty enough, your puppy might not be hungry (try and train him on an empty stomach), he might be too stressed or he might get his treats all the time so he doesn't realize what the reward means.

Over reinforcement, which simply means using treats too often, is common.

This is why, over time, you will reduce the value of the treat as he learns the desired behavior, and reward based on the quality of the response and then scale back the value here too.

You are eventually aiming to have the desired behavior with no treats at all (you won't always be able to have a treat in your hand) but you will always praise your dog for returning to you and you may also have a reward game for him to play (a tug or a ball to throw).

The reward might not always be a treat and it doesn't need to be. A dog can never have too much love or too much play.

Dogs train better when they are making their own choices and you want him to want to make the choice to come to you when you ask him. This means that you must never be angry when he comes back to you, no matter how long it has taken.

. . .

Harness

Collars and choke collars are no longer thought to be good for dogs. They can be worn in the house but harnesses should be used for training - especially leash and recall. Training is all about trust and restrictive items just won't build the trust you are looking for.

If your puppy jumps around when you try to get the harness on him, a trick is to begin by holding a treat through the opening of his harness where you need his head to go and encourage him to put his head through to get the treat. You need to deal with his legs so ask him to sit as you do this.

I use 'sit' and 'wait' as I pull the straps around his chest and under his legs. He usually stands (I just use the 'wait' cue for this part) for the lower strap. He just seems to find this more comfortable.

Reward each step and success and take it slowly.

Leash

Avoid flexible leashes. They won't give you the control that you need and they won't be strong enough for your GSD. A 4ft leash can work well as both a training and a day leash.

You will ideally want to use a long-leash too (around 25ft-30ft in length). This is known as a long-line and you may also want a shorter training leash. His day-leash or 'normal' leash will be shorter than the training leash.

Whistles and Clickers

Almost all leash training will involve using a clicker - I train with and without a clicker. Whistles are great for recall especially for dog breeds that like to explore.

With clicker training, this must always be followed with a reward, for example, click-treat. This is known as the primary and secondary enforcer.

Eventually, you will click less and less as the behavior is established but you must always follow a click with a treat.

Toys

You are going to use your puppy's toys during the recall training. You are going to try to get him to leave a toy and come to you when he is called. You will have a treat so that he sees the value of leaving his toy and coming to get something else he loves.

If you are training a gun dog for retrieval then you can get lots of scent items such as rabbit scent balls and puppy dummies. We once trained a spaniel by scenting a sock with a pheasant and hiding it for them to find when asked to fetch.

Basic Training

In the first few weeks that your puppy is home, there is some basic training that you can start right away that can teach him some of the basic commands that you will use throughout his life.

Always keep the training sessions between 5 and 10 minutes. If he comes up against something he can't do, then return to something that he can do so that you can praise and reward him at the end of the training session.

I mention using hand signals during some of the basics described below and you should try to use this type of training as much as your can rather than just verbal cues.

Try your best to use both if you don't feel comfortable with only hand signals.

This is the same for using treats as rewards. Try to reward

without a treat by using praise or other forms of reinforcement if you can.

Reinforcement (a part of operant conditioning) and using body language rather than verbal cues is now considered as the foundation for good dog training.

Getting to know his name

Always reward your puppy when he responds to his name.

It doesn't matter how or why he responds to his name; it only matters that he is and that you need to reward him for doing so. This might be harder to do when he is chewing something that he shouldn't be.

Don't ever be tempted to use his name as punishment. He won't understand and will be confused by your use of his name and confused by your behavior and annoyance.

Look at Me

Before you start taking your puppy outside for walks you will want to teach him to look at you. To do this he needs to want to pay attention to you.

Simply reward him every time he looks at you and repeat the process in many different locations and environments. You can reward him with click-treat, with praise and reward and the reward might be some play or a toy (spaniels love a ball throw).

Training your puppy to look at you can be done with an easy game and it will teach your puppy to look and also get him used to his name.

To play the game, sit down with your puppy with a handful of treats in your pocket. Make sure that you are sitting so that you are close to him but that he needs to look up to see your eyes.

Take out a treat and get his attention. Place the treat

between your eyes. Your puppy will follow the treat all the way to your head and eyes. As soon as there is eye-contact, even briefly, give him his treat.

In the beginning, the eye contact might be an accident on his part but that's okay. If he gets rewarded for it, he will soon learn. Keep repeating until he always has eye contact with you.

Keep doing this and then start putting the treat behind your head or neck but try and get eye contact before you give him his treat. If he doesn't look at you at first, then help him find your eyes so that he knows what he is supposed to do.

The next part of this game is to start using his name. Do exactly the same process but as you place the treat between your eyes, say his name. You will need to do all this quite quickly to link the eye contact and name call with his reward but he will get there.

He now knows that when you say his name you want him to look at you and to pay attention to you because there will be a reward coming!

Teach him to Sit

There are a few ways to teach your puppy to sit, but I have used this one to the best effect.

Sit down beside your puppy holding a treat, then put the treat in front of his nose, slowly lifting it above his head. As he tilts his head to follow the treat, he is likely to sit as he tries to reach the treat.

I would usually say the word 'sit' just before his bottom touches the ground. Then, as soon as his bottom touches the ground, reward him with the treat. Your puppy is learning the word sit but also starting to recognize your hand, signal.

Keep doing this, eventually removing the treat from your hand but using your hand as a signal or cue to get him to sit and saying the word 'sit' as you start to raise your hand to the sitting position. Always reward him as soon as he sits down.

The other way to teach him to sit seems to be something that kids are really good at teaching.

Just stand in front of your puppy with his treats and ask him to sit. Then wait for him to sit, and as soon as he does, reward him with praise and a treat.

Next, move away from your position so that he needs to stand up, then repeat. After a few successful attempts, begin using the word 'sit' as he starts to get into position, rewarding him all the time. Don't try to push his bottom to the ground to get him to sit - it rarely works.

Teach him to Lie Down

For some reason, this can be the fastest command to teach your puppy and he might even be lying down within one or two training sessions.

Simply take out his treat and hold it to his nose, then move it down slowly to the floor (I usually say 'Lie Down' at this point too rather than wait until later in training). Slide the treat on the floor away from him if you need to because this will make him start to move down naturally.

As soon as he is almost down (he won't lie down right away, and his bottom is likely to remain in mid-air), gave him the treat. Keep doing this and getting him to move further into the lie position (you can keep dragging the treat towards you on the floor to help him get into the correct position).

Reward and praise him each time. Eventually, you will only give him the treat when he is fully down. By now, he will be used to your hand moving down and hearing the phrase 'Lie Down.'

Teach him to stay or wait

You can use either term with your puppy. I use both but in different circumstances. For example, I use 'wait' when we are crossing a road, and I want him to wait before I cue that it's ok to move.

On the other hand, I use 'stay' if someone comes to the door and I don't want him running into the hall. You can use the same command for both of these.

To teach your dog to stay, first of all, ask him to sit. Then hold up your hand so that your palm is straight in front of him and directed towards his face (but not in any kind of threatening way).

Take a step backward so that you are facing him with your palm facing him and say stay. If he stays for even a few seconds, come back to him and reward him.

Keep doing this while moving further away.

Leash training

As soon as his leash is clipped on, give him a treat. Have a treat in your hand and use this to get him to walk beside you.

Hold it just in front of his nose, loosely cupped in your hand so that your palm is facing his nose with your arm hanging down beside you.

He will eventually be running beside you, or more precisely, running after your hand. Build this up slowly and for no more than 5 minutes at a time at the start.

Eventually, walk a few paces, then turn in the opposite direction getting him to follow you.

Repeat this process of walking a few steps and turning.

11

THE FOUNDATIONAL CUES

You are aiming to have your dog return to you on cue no matter how many other exciting things are going on around him.

This means that you want your puppy to want to return to you on cue, not only when there are no other dogs around, but also when there are dogs to play with.

You can only achieve this if you are more interesting than whatever else he is doing, and if he is listening, and paying attention to you.

In summary, you want him to stop what he is doing; you want him to look at you, and you want him to come to you on cue.

Like many things with training, it takes a little bit of time. Ideally, you want your dog to automatically return to you whenever he feels threatened. This means any bad situation can be avoided before it even begins.

Sit, stay is an important part of recall training and it's an important part of overall behavior. Ideally, every time he sees another dog, you will want to get him to come to you and sit and stay.

You will start the recall and 'sit stay' training at home, and you won't let him off leash outside in an unenclosed area until you are happy that he will return to you, and that he is already doing what you want him to do in the home or the garden.

To do this you, need to introduce different locations and then introduce lots of distractions as the training develops, because there will be lots of exciting activity and scents in the park, but wait until his recall is up to about 70%-80% before you start adding the distraction element of his recall training.

Decide on your cue

Most people use the word 'come' or 'here' as their vocal cue for their dog. Once you have decided on the word you want to use, then you must keep it. Consistency is vital for your dog to understand what you mean.

You will start using this early. When you want him to come for his dinner you will use it, when you are going to give him a big cuddle or play with him, you will use it.

The word itself doesn't mean anything to your dog, but the outcome of his action means he feels great and gets something he loves.

In training language, he is building a positive association with the word. Try to build in hand signals too - I tend to open my arms as a visual cue to come.

Like most training sessions, keep the training to around 10 minutes and watch out for any signs that he is getting stressed (quick head movements, grabbing the treat/food, ears flat) and try not to get over-excited.

If your puppy is a part of a household then get all members involved in the training too. At the end of his training get him to do something you know he can do so that it ends in success. You want him to enjoy his training.

Sit Stay and Release

Sit Stay is one of the most important cues your dog will learn. Dogs naturally want to follow you, especially as you move away from them.

You will want to use both verbal and visual cues. Your visual cue will be holding up your hand, but without raising your arm - just hold it in front of you and direct your palm to your puppy's face. This is his visual cue for stay.

The verbal cue would be 'Stay'. Visual cues are also a good way of helping your dog focus on you.

Normally the first part is to ask your puppy to 'sit' then this is followed by 'stay' (or 'wait').

By this stage (by the time you are going for outside walks) you will have trained your puppy to 'sit' and will have practiced some 'stay' in the home or garden.

To recap on the 'sit' training. Never force your puppy to sit by putting your hand on his lower back and pushing it down.

Decide on your visual signal for sit. An example would be to hold out your hand palm facing-up, then gently move your fingers upwards as if you are 'lifting' his head with your four fingers.

Take out a treat and bring it towards your puppy's nose slowly moving it up over his head so that he naturally goes into a sit position.

As soon as his bottom touches the ground praise him and give him the treat. If you are clicker training then use the clicker as his bottom touches the ground and provide the treat.

Try to make sure that you provide the praise/treat when he is sitting and not when he has moved to a standing position.

Whenever you see your puppy sit praise and reward him (with voice or clicker - click-treat) and then start introducing the verbal cue. You can start the verbal cue earlier, for example, say the cue 'sit' right before his bottom touches the ground and he is due to receive his praise/reward.

Every time after that, when your puppy sits try and remember to praise/reward them as this will build this into a behavior default. One that they enjoy and know brings praise/reward and they are comfortable and safe with.

You will want your puppy to sit for lots of reasons. In the car, when you go the door, at a crosswalk, and so on. This means you need to train him to sit but you also need to let him know when it's okay to move forward.

To do this, first of all, have him on his leash. Get him to sit (and reward) then decide on your cue for 'let's go' this can be 'let's go' or 'ok go' or whatever you choose. Say your cue and move a few steps and praise him, ask him to sit and reward.

Begin with short distances (a few steps) to get him used to the 'ok go' cue. Repeat the process of 'sit', reward 'ok go' reward, walk a few steps then repeat. This is known as the release command or release cue.

This can mean that the release cue is seen as a reward too because when he comes back he then gets to go and have fun again. It also means that he will learn that coming back doesn't mean the end of the play.

Finally, some trainers consider recall to include holding your puppy's collar when he returns as full recall and used before the release cue. The puppy comes back, he sits and the collar is taken then the reward is given. This is followed by the release cue.

Some are happy with only the sit. This really is up to you but I prefer the collar hold as it gives you more control should you ever need it.

Other behaviors

Interruption and distraction are great ways to prevent many behaviours that you don't want as we have seen in the previous chapters.

If you see your puppy or dog behaving in a way that you don't want or, specifically, if you can see he is about to, then use distract or interrupt his attention.

You can do this by using a sound or a cue or turning and walking in a different direction (this is particularly useful if you see him reacting to other dogs or dogs that might bot read his signals to leave him alone).

JUMPING Up

All dogs like to try and jump up but, due to the size of your German Shepherd as he gets older, you will need to train him to prevent this as soon as you start to see it.

If he jumps up on you you say 'Down' and then turn your back on him. If this doesn't work you can also try raising your knee to make it difficult for him - just ensure that you don't connect with him or hurt him in the process. You only want to block his efforts.

DROP IT/LEAVE it

This is great command and can be used when paying ball, frisbee, or if you need him to drop something that you don't want him to have in his mouth.

It will takes a few lessons but the easiest way is to offer a treat for a ball drop and lots of praise as he releases the ball in order to receive his treat. Say 'Drop It' or 'Leave It', present his treat, when he drops the ball, praise and reward.

12

RECALL TRAINING

You will begin teaching your puppy what you mean by the recall cue. I will use the example of 'come'. The important part is to always use this word and use it only when you want him to come to you. Don't mix it into other cues. This one word means one thing, and one thing only - to come to you.

You will adopt this rule for all his cues. Make sure each one is unique to the action expected and not mixed into other meanings or cues. For example, don't use 'come here' if 'here' is used as another cue.

Start your recall training in the house then move to enclosed areas with few distractions.

I know of someone who trained for recall in their hallway, which was ideal for ensuring their puppy was set up for success during the early training because there were limited directional options, and little distraction. This is important.

You want to ensure that your puppy always succeeds and this might mean you need to adapt things to make sure that he can succeed through each step of his training.

Get him used to coming to you

Once you have decided on your location, show your puppy his favorite treat or toy, and as he comes towards you to get his toy or treat (don't ask him to just let him do it by himself), praise him and reward him as he reaches you. Do this a few times.

After a few times start to add in his cue so that he gets used to it. As he starts coming towards you to get his toy (and ideally looks at you), add in the cue you have chosen. In my example, 'Come'.

Once he is doing this you can add in a sit.

As soon as he comes to you give him his treat and ask him to sit. When he sits give him another reward.

You then want to keep repeating this game in other rooms of the house and with more distractions.

One way to do this is to have other family members or friends in the room. As you walk towards them and he starts to get interested in this interesting and fun distraction, quickly run away and call him so that he chases you.

Encourage him to catch up and when he does, he will of course get his treat and probably a big cuddle as an extra reward.

Like many of the games you can play with him, mix them up so that he doesn't always know what to expect. It will keep him even more interested in what you are about to get up to next.

10 steps for basic recall

1. Decide on your location (hallway, kitchen, etc)
2. Show your puppy his favorite toy or a treat but don't call him, let him come to you
3. When he gets to you give him his reward.
4. Repeat

5. Start adding your recall cue as he starts coming towards you
6. Reward him when he gets to you
7. Repeat steps 5 and 6
8. When he comes to you give him his treat then ask him to sit and give him another treat
9. Repeat this until he knows what to do
10. Repeat the recall and sit training in other locations and start to add in distractions

Training sit-stay

Ask your puppy to sit, then 'stay' and still facing him, take a few steps backward holding up your hand in the 'stay' position. Walk back to your puppy and reward him.

Do this a few times and then take a few more steps backward increasing the distance then walk back to him and reward him. Keep repeating moving further away.

Your puppy is learning that not only is he getting rewarded but that you come back to him. Start to move to different positions so that you are to each side and eventually behind him. If he gets up, just move back to him and give him praise then try again.

You will need to repeat this in several different locations not only in one room or in your own garden. As he starts to get better at this begin to introduce him to areas with more distractions and start moving behind objects so that he can't see you. Try and do this everywhere you go.

Sit stay come

This was the main recall training I started with Millie indoors when she was around 14 weeks old and it was very effective.

Ask your puppy to sit and then asked her to stay as above (I used the word 'wait' and held my hand up).

Walk backward a few steps facing your puppy - I kept holding my hand up as I was walking away.

The difference now is that you want him to come to you following the sit-stay. If he stays for just a few seconds, ask him to come and give him a treat and be delighted with him.

Keep repeating this and do it at the start of every training session. As he starts to get good at this, start to move further and further away and eventually try walking away with your back to him.

Build up distance and distractions to this game - but if you go too far and he starts to come towards you too soon, just go back a few steps to the point at which it was working and then keep trying to build the distance.

The next stage is to go outside but not for a 'proper' walk just yet. You can go for a walk on-leash but not off-leash.

Going Outside - enclosed area

Training for recall outside of the house is vital. It is here where he is going to find the most distractions. You must make sure the area you choose in enclosed. Just like the early days of house training, you will start with very few distractions.

This is when you are going to work with the clicker and training leads and when you will start working out the value that he attaches to each of his different treats.

A great tip is to train your puppy before he has eaten - this means the treat you are offering will be of higher value to him and he will be more interested in them! And don't train him for too long. Pay attention if he looks like he is getting bored and stop the training and start again the next day.

You also want him to know that coming to you is more

rewarding than doing something else - it is exciting and fun and may involve a tasty treat.

I also used to crouch down and hold my arms wide as Barney ran to me when he was a puppy. It wasn't meant as a signal but even today if I hold my arms wide, he will come to me.

To get started, put your puppy in his harness and on his training leash. Just like the early indoor training, you can start with rewarding an action with no other cues, to get him used to the long-line and outdoor training. He will know what to do quickly, because he has already been trained indoors.

The difference now is that you are going to place something he might want to eat or go to, a short distance away from him, and within the length of the leash, or just a bit further away. You are now introducing something he wants to get to, that is away from you.

As he goes towards the object or the treat (but not too tasty), tighten his leash and say his name then the cue e.g., Barney 'come'. As soon as he turns and comes (only a step or two) reward and praise him.

If you are using a clicker, you will click as soon as he turns (there is more on clicker training later). Aim to have an even tastier treat for him than the one he was going towards.

You want to increase the value of the treats the more you want him to do something, so that he prefers to choose that treat.

By having the leash on him, you can also gently encourage him to come towards you to get his reward if you need to. The leash helps you have a bit of control over this recall in the early stages as he learns the cue 'come' outside of the house, and where he will want to explore.

You will also play on the training leash and long line. Give him a few treats then run forward or backward a few steps and say 'Barney, Come!' in a playful voice. Hold the treat out at the height of his nose (so that all of his feet are on the ground) and as he reaches you give him his treat.

You can extend this game to add the sit. As he reaches you for his treat, move the treat up in front of his nose, so that he is forced back into a sit position to get his treat.

In this way the come and sit are the same cue which means when you ask him to come, he will come to you and sit without being asked to sit.

You can, and should start practicing this as soon as you can. Puppies learn most up to the age of 18 weeks.

The next step for recall training is to have him move further away from you, and for him to return when he hears his cue. Good recall means he does this all the time. If he is not, then he is not ready, and you won't want to risk letting him off-leash.

To understand what you are asking your puppy to do, think about it like this. He is exploring and having fun, he is finding interesting and exciting things to sniff and play with.

When you call him, you want him to prefer to come to you rather than to do whatever he is doing. If you can achieve this, then there is no reason for him not to return to you when called.

To do this you will want to start with training games, and you will have worked out what his favorite treats are, and which ones top the list. Cheese, hotdog, carrot, kibble for example.

Using the long-line

You don't need to use the long-line but it can be really helpful and, if you can, I would recommend it. To describe how this is done I picked a hand but you will end up doing something that works for you.

Practice this in a garden if you can, and, in the beginning, have no other distractions. You want to get used to working with the long line and you also want to test that your training is working.

Hold the end of the line in your right hand so that you have it tightly held. Wrap the length of the line into loops so that you can slowly release the line over the front of your body, feeding it through your left hand, making sure it can be easily released.

In your left hand, you are holding the part of the line that is acting as your dog leash, and it is attached to his harness, but your hand is operating as a feeder, controlling the delivery of the line.

This means you can slowly release the line through your left hand, to allow your puppy to move away from you, or clamp it closed (gently) to stop further release of the line.

You will have your right hand holding the end of the long line as well as the loops of the spare line.

Once you are comfortable you can start the training.

Slowly move in a circle on the same spot so that he is running around you, loosening the line so that he can move away from you, and then call him back to you. Just get him used to the leash and watching you, and knowing that he gets a reward when he comes back.

You can then add another game (and later you can play this off-leash too), by throwing a treat away from you, and letting your puppy go towards the treat.

Once he has eaten his treat, call his name to get his attention, and wait until he looks at you (click), 'come' (cue), and when he comes to you (praise/reward). Then throw another treat in a different direction so that he constantly running away and towards you in a fun game.

When you need to tighten or 'pull' the line to encourage him to come back on his cue, move or lean forward rather than move against him, and gently make the line shorter. This allows you to be in control of your puppy whilst letting him return without feeling 'pulled'.

The final part is to wait until he is preoccupied with something and is not looking at you. Get his attention and ask him to come.

If he comes then praise and reward. If he doesn't come, just walk to him and show him all the treats you have, and then walk away from him.

He is likely to follow you to try and get a treat. Just ignore him. As soon as he is not right beside you, ask him to come. When he does, give him lots of praise and a favorite treat. It won't take long for him to realize that coming is much better than not coming.

The next step is to repeat the indoor sit stay come training in the outdoor environment. Just as you did indoors get your puppy to sit-stay and then move away from him while still facing him and then ask him to 'come'. e.g., 'Barney, come'. Slowly build the distance all the while using the long line.

The next two steps are new, and before you can try off-leash outdoor you want to introduce the 'let's go' or 'let's play' cue which combines the sit-stay.

Ask him to sit-stay beside you, then use your release cue, 'let's go', and start walking. As he moves away and then moves ahead of you, call him back to you (click on a turn of the head towards you), as he starts coming towards you might want to encourage him (I held my arms open), reward him when he gets to you, then ask him to sit (reward).

The last step is to practice off-leash - again, you will do this in a space that is enclosed and where he will be safe. Simply let him wander away from you and then call him to you using your cue. Be exciting and have a treat ready for him. Try and keep his attention on you as he comes to you - make a noise or hold your arms open - you want him to be focused on you.

Don't keep repeating the cue or start raising your voice if he doesn't come. This will confuse him, and he won't be able to understand what his cue word is, eventually tuning it out which means he just won't hear it.

If you raise your voice, he won't think that coming to you is going to be lots of fun. Eventually, it could have the opposite effect, and he won't want to come at all.

The best way to train your puppy is using random and variable reinforcement. All this means is that over time change how often he gets a treat for the same behavior, so that he is hoping for it each time (don't wait too long to reward as you start to reduce the level of treats) and change the value of the treat (for a really good response).

If you want to, you can measure the average response time for recall (either daily or per 12 returns, etc.) so that when he comes back faster, he gets a super tasty treat. This is the most effective way to train your puppy to become addicted to coming back to you.

One last trick - if your puppy has taken a while to return on cue then, when he arrives, show him the treat and put it back in your pocket. As he moves away ask him to 'come' and, when he gets to you, give him his treat. This will help him learn that acting right away gets the reward.

Using a Clicker

Clicker training is useful when you want to mark the correct behaviour of your puppy at the exact moment he starts to respond. As I have already mentioned, if you are doing click-reward then it must always be followed by a reward, but the reward and the timing of the reward varies.

In the beginning, all you need to do is get your puppy used to the click-reward (at the start you will use a treat). Keep repeating click-treat. He doesn't have to do anything at this stage as you are just getting him used to the clicker marker which means a reward is coming.

Slowly reduce the time between the click and the treat and vary the gaps - he will still expect the treat and he will know that it is coming, but that it might not happen right away.

Once he gets good at this, you will be able to click without the treat, and vary the reinforcement by using his favorite toy or a quick game that he likes.

For example, when you call his name and he begins to start coming towards you, you can click so that he knows a reward is coming. It helps to keep him motivated to come all the way back to you in the expectation of a good time when he gets there.

Recall Summary and where the Clicker fits in

The process for recall training is as follows:

1. Call your dog

Say "Barney", "Come" (cue - or use a whistle cue)

2. When he comes ask him to "Sit" (cue). Take his collar and praise him and reward

3. Release him "Ok Go" (cue)

If you are using a clicker as a marker then the full process would look like this:

1. Get your puppy to come to you

Start by throwing a treat away from you then throw a treat at your feet. Reward every time your puppy comes back to you for any reason. You can add the click with your clicker to mark as soon as he turns towards you.

2. Add a cue

As your puppy turns towards you, again, this is for any reason, add your recall cue and your click (if you are using a clicker to mark or capture the behavior). The recall cue can be 'come', 'here' or a whistle - either your own whistle or use a plastic one.

Practice at different locations and over different distances before you move to the next step.

3. As soon as your puppy looks towards you click and add the recall cue. As you are walking on the leash vary the length. Every time he looks towards you, click and then add the recall cue (and don't forget the reward).

4. You will now cue him to look and come to you. With your puppy walking in front of you say (or whistle) your cue, as he turns towards you add the click marker. Practice by varying the distance and the speed the dog is moving away.

5. If you want to add a sit then this is when you will add it to your training.

When he arrives back to you use your sit cue to get him to sit. As soon as he sits add a click and then the reward.

6. Add a collar hold. You can train this separately or you can add it into the recall process here.

When he has arrived back and sits, lean in and take hold of his collar - as you do this use your clicker to mark then reward.

Once he is good and is succeeding with steps 1 to 6 you can start adding in distractions.

You will start with low-level distractions and build them up to higher-value distractions.

Distractions might be kibble, bread, eggs, cheese, meat, and toys (again in order of least to most favorite).

As he moves towards the distraction e.g., the bread, start your recall with your recall cue, and the click-reward process above. If he fails then reduce the value of the distraction until he is succeeding.

In terms of what distractions might be, then this can be a dog he knows, a dog he doesn't know (high-value distraction), someone he knows, a group of people, a jogger, a bicycle an old scent, and the high-value new scent (a squirrel that you have noticed running up a tree).

Try and remember to complete a sequence. Try to always

have your dog notice you (click), come to you (encouragement) arrive (treat), sit (treat), collar hold (treat), 'go play' (reward). This is much more rewarding than 'come', treat, end of the game.

By continuing to reward after he comes back to you, by rewarding the sit, collar hold and then releasing with a 'go play' cue, he will have the expectation of more exciting things to come than if the rewards ended with the return cue only.

He also knows that he can return to playing after if he comes back to you and receives all his rewards. Don't forget that the 'go play' cue is a reward in itself.

This will become even more useful once you start going outdoors to parks and other walks where there are even more exciting distractions and ones that you are not in control of.

Proofing

Proofing is when you want to prove to yourself that the training has worked. You will proof before you let your puppy off-leash.

To do this, you will create distractions and then aim to get him to come to you on cue.

You should also proof around other dogs. Try and arrange a play-date with at least one other dog and then while he is playing with them (and still on the long-line) call him to you. Make sure you have a very tasty treat and be full of praise when he comes to you.

Once he comes to you and receives his reward he is released to his cue, such as 'let's go', to play again. As already mentioned, this particular activity is also useful to teach him that coming to you doesn't mean the end of the playtime.

The last step is to practice off-leash - again, you will do this in a space that is enclosed and where he will be safe. Simply let him wander away from you and then call him to you using your cue. Be exciting and have a treat ready for him.

Don't keep repeating the cue if he doesn't come or start raising your voice. This will confuse him and he won't be able to understand what his cue word is.

If you raise your voice, he won't think that coming to you is going to be lots of fun and, as noted earlier, it can lead to having the opposite effect and he won't want to come at all.

If he isn't coming to you as you go through all the training you have already completed go back to the long line until you are sure he understands what you are asking him to do.

Emergency stop

Training for an emergency stop can be one aspect of recall that saves your dog's life. It is also quite easy to train especially once you have been working on recall training.

First of all, you will want to use a specific cue. This can be any word but, again, it can only have one meaning. The most common word that is used is 'Stop'. Just make sure this is not used as a part of any other cue.

To begin with, have your puppy or dog sitting in front of you and have a treat in your hand. If your dog is not food orientated try using one of his toys.

Take a step back, put your arm in the air as if you are trying to stop the traffic or saying hello to someone who is a distance away. This is important as it is more likely that your emergency stop signal will be visual and not sound-based (call or whistle) when your dog is a distance away from you.

Raise your arm with the treat in your hand, say the word 'Stop', and then throw the treat over your dog's head towards his rear from your raised hand so that the treat falls behind him or just beside him. You want to make sure that your dog needs to turn around to get the treat.

As he starts to return to you, repeat by putting your arm in the air, saying Stop and throwing another treat over his head. This will force him to stop to turn around to get the treat.

You will notice that he starts to pay attention to you and your hand, which is what you want him to do.

Once he is paying attention, stopping and turning to get the treat as you raise your arm, you can think about increasing the distance. If there are any problems with the next step return to this first stage.

You will now start throwing the treat a bit further away so that there is a bigger distance between you so that when you say Stop, put your arm in the air, and throw the treat over his head, he is not close to you. This is how you can build up the long-distance emergency stop.

Try to make sure the treat doesn't land in front of him because you want him to turn around to get the treat. You want him to do this because it stops his forward movement. Keep building up the distance and repeating the exercise.

You want to reach the point where, with your arm in the air, you say Stop, he looks towards you and stops. If he starts to come towards you, go back to the first step and reinforce the stop when he is right in front of you.

If your dog is a fast learner it may take a few days but this can take a few weeks so just be patient.

The very last step is when you don't throw the treat at the end but instead, walk towards him to give him his reward. This is because, if you are in a park and he is far away you won't be able to throw a treat behind him. The final part of the training is letting him know a reward is coming.

What not to do

If your dog does not return to you when you call him simply go and retrieve him and put him on his leash. Don't be angry with him, simply put him on the leash, and move him away from whatever it is that is distracting him. This, in itself, lets him know that coming back is a much better option.

Don't keep calling the same cue over and over again. For example, if he does not come when you call and you keep repeating the cue louder and louder the cue itself will lose its value and your puppy will simply tune it out as noise. If your cue isn't working then choose a new one and train your puppy to know what it is.

Don't have only one person training him if he lives with other family members. If your puppy is a family dog then everyone needs to be involved in the training, and everyone needs to use the same cues. Ideally, everyone should be involved in the daily training, even for just a few minutes.

Never punish your puppy when he fails. This is particularly important with recall (and with separation anxiety).

If you get angry with them, or punish them, when they finally return to you after not coming back right away, all he will learn is that coming back to you is not a good experience and that it has negative consequences. It is not fun. All this will do is make his recall worse, not better.

Don't use the "come" cue of your dog if fully focused on something else and is unlikely to hear you.

In this case, use his name to get his attention and to check that he can hear you (does he react by turning slightly towards you or twitch his ear). If he does, then use his "come" cue.

If he is far away you can use a whistle or whistle yourself, and if he can see you use your hand signal - in Barney's case this is wide open arms.

Only use your "come" cue if you think it is likely to succeed. If you call and he does not come, walk to him. Don't give him into trouble or reward him.

If he does not 'come' you know he is not fully trained so re-start the training to the point he was succeeding, and build it up again from there.

Finally, do no use the recall cue for things they might not like doing. For example, don't associate it with a bath, or getting groomed, or having a tick removed if your puppy doesn't like these things.

The main point is that you need your puppy to associate your recall cue "come", with something he is going to like.

13

GOING TO THE PARK

Once you are ready to move to the park where you will encounter even more distractions, you will want to begin with using high value (or higher value) treats than you have been using indoors and in the enclosed area.

It is going to be harder for him to return, and therefore you want the reward to be extra special. You will also vary these treats so he doesn't know what to expect but he knows a really tasty treat is coming.

You might also want to vary the timing of the treat so he knows it's coming and it will be tasty but it might be in 1, 2, or 5 seconds (you will want to start varying the immediacy of the reward when you are doing the outdoor enclosed training).

Try not to only call your dog to you at the end of his walk. If you do it throughout the walk and reward him each time he comes back, he won't associate recall with the end of playtime.

At the end of the walk, make coming back fun and rewarding rather than something he doesn't like. I tend to play more at the end of the walk as I return to the entry gate of the park.

During the walk, you can vary his treat reward depending on how well he comes back to you when you give him his recall cue. If you call, and he continues to do what he is doing for a minute or two and then comes back, don't reward him right away.

Let him smell his treat and then let him start to move away from you. Call him again quickly (you want him to be set up to succeed, he needs to know what you want him to), and if he immediately turns around and comes back then reward and praise him. He will then be able to learn exactly what you mean, and what you want from him, when you give him his recall cue.

In the early stages, try rewarding him with one of his less favorite treats rather than no reward at all for taking his time to come back. You want to ensure that he doesn't think he is being punished (by not getting his treat) for coming back, even if he took his time about it.

But remember, if you have already established a connection with your puppy and he finds you interesting, this will be much easier.

You can take your puppy to the park on a long line but never let him off-leash until you are confident of his recall. You can let go of the long leash and if he runs too far you can stand on the end of it. It is much easier to do this than try and grab a shorter lead.

As you start to venture out on walks, your puppy won't be the only one meeting other similar animals to talk and play with.

It's important to pay attention to your puppy and to keep playing with him, and being fun, during a walk too. Standing around and talking to other dog walkers and ignoring him will mean, although he might be well exercised through all his running around, he is learning that you are not the most exciting thing in his life and his attention to you (and your recall cue) may not be 'heard'. He will simply tune it out as his attention is elsewhere.

Other dogs and their communication signals

The first thing that is going to happen when you can take your puppy out for real walks after his required vaccinations, is that he is going to meet other dogs the you both don't know.

Your puppy is going to be playful and excited to meet other dogs, but these dogs may not be so eager to have an excited puppy trying to play with them.

Older dogs (those over 2 years old) are not likely to want to play - in fact - dogs over 2 years old will tend to only play with dogs they know. Many will stop playing with other dogs altogether. Both Millie and Barney don't play with other dogs anymore, they run along together or play with their balls or sticks.

You will also need to pay attention to how the dogs you meet are reacting. Dogs will tell you far in advance if they are getting annoyed, are uncomfortable or feel threatened. I don't know how many times I have seen the owner of a dog watch as his dog tries to get another dog to play, and the dog being approached tries, again and again, to say 'no' until eventually, it runs out of options and snaps or even tries to bite to the dog who is pestering it.

These are the general stages to watch out for, and this will be the case both for your dog, and for the dogs that you meet. Try to pay attention to what dogs are telling each other and telling us.

If a dog is displaying this behavior, then these are signs that he is feeling threatened, and is not happy with the attention of another dog, when it is close to him: -

Stage 1: Yawning, looking away, licking lips, moving away

Stage 2: Panting, hackles up, and whale eyes (when a dog shows the whites of his eyes). This is a clear warning signal. If this still doesn't work then the next part will be a lip curl or snarl

Stage 3: Lip curl or snarl or growl and possibly a snap. Then finally we will reach the stage we don't want to be

Stage 4: A lunge towards the other dog (or the source of the 'threat') with barking as your dog tries to make the threat go away and then this may be followed by a bite.

How dogs greet each other

You need to be aware of other dogs, and, when you meet them, watch and understand what they are saying.

A dog running at another dog is not going to go down well. I am still surprised how often I see dog owners letting their dogs do this. Both Millie and Barney are friendly dogs but they hate it. If you see a dog running towards your puppy or dog, then there are a few things you can do.

As soon as I see this happening, and depending on how far away the other dog is, and how fast they are running, I will throw a ball or a stick to distract Millie and Barney. This can sometimes encourage the other dog as well, and if I notice this, I just ignore the other dog and turn away with Millie and Barney in the opposite direction. If Barney is playing further away from me, and he feels threatened by another dog, he comes back to me to be safe. If a dog runs towards him, he comes as close as he can - he sometimes tries to jump up into my arms.

Millie tends to feel less threatened and seems to find it easier to deal with other dogs without resorting to aggression or fear. She must communicate well! She does this by a lip curl, then a growl, sometimes she adds in a whale eye, then an air snap but all of this is extremely unusual and she needs a lot of provocation. She always, like most dogs, starts with avoidance of the other dog if she can.

Others signs to watch out for include tails, are the tails up, and are the hackles up? Neither necessarily mean that the dog is aggressive but it indicates high adrenaline. If you notice this, distract your puppy or dog away from the other dog.

Two dogs that meet each other head-on and stare into each other's faces are not being friendly, but a dog that approaches from the side is being polite and asking for the intrusion into your dog's space.

A face greeting followed by a bottom sniff tends to be friendly. Bottom sniffing, generally, is fine and nothing to worry about.

If another dog puts his head across another dogs' shoulders this can be a sign of aggression and it can often be followed by mounting.

Just remember to always ask the other dog owner if it is ok for your puppy or dog to play with their dog. Do this especially if their dog is on a leash. Don't forget a dog that is on a leash might feel threatened by another dog, who is not on a leash, and who then tries to play with him. The dog on the leash will feel constrained, and this can lead to anxiety and a reaction to defend himself.

All of this is very important as your puppy begins his first walks. The experiences he has with other dogs at this stage are vital to how he views other dogs in the future, and if his experience is negative then he can easily build a negative association with other dogs - and be aggressive himself (he would see them as a threat).

One of the ways that you can help keep your puppy from getting over-excited around other dogs is to be more exciting yourself! Of course, you can also teach him sit-stay. Every time he sees another dog you will want to get him to sit and stay (and reward and praise him at each stage as he learns this). You can use a clicker if you wish, and every time he learns a little bit more, click and reward.

As you first start to take your puppy out, he is likely to want to run up to other dogs himself. This is very different as it will be clear to most dogs that he is not being aggressive but curious and playful.

However, and as noted earlier, dogs older than 2 years old don't tend to like being harassed by a puppy so just make sure you don't create a situation that then leads your puppy to start fearing other dogs. Millie, who is now 11 years old and has been a mum herself, will persevere with a puppy for a few minutes but she will then let it know to leave her alone. Barney (now 5 years old) will try to completely ignore a puppy for as long as he can.

However, puppies learn by meeting other dogs and learning not to bother them, so try and teach them the basics with a dog you know.

How to interact with humans

You will already know some of these but a couple of points are worth re-stating. Don't let a stranger pat your puppy or dog on the head. They can bring their hand slowly towards them from the side so he can sniff the hand.

If your puppy starts to back away this is a sign of fear, and an early communication, so try to notice it and don't ignore it.

If your puppy starts to yawn, or lick his lips, then this is the next level of communication, and he is really trying to tell you and the other person that he is uncomfortable.

The final warning will be a bark. He will only get to this stage if nothing else has worked.

The best way to try and teach him that someone is not to be feared is to reward your puppy when he sees them to create a positive association. You can also try showing your puppy that there is nothing to fear by touching, perhaps shaking a hand, and quietly talking, and while you are doing this, reward with a high-value treat.

Games

German Shepherds love exercise and they need both physical and mental exercise.

When he is a puppy you will only be walking him for around 20 minutes at a time and around 4 times per day. Don't be tempted to over-exercise him because this is not good for him (and try and prevent too many high impact games like jumping for a frisbee too often at this stage of his development).

You will use games for lots of reasons. One of the things you want to get your puppy to do is to watch you and know where you are. You always want to be moving around so that he knows he needs to keep an eye on you.

Hide and go seek is a great game to play. I love it more than the dogs and you probably will too.

This is game teaches them to pay attention to you. If you have forgotten how to play, hide behind a tree or a wall or any object. Let him run over to you and then come out, praise him and give him his treat.

A good way to play a game that reinforces paying attention to you (and can help remove any anxiety if other dogs are approaching) is to have them walk slightly in front of you and throw a really nice (and smelly) treat near you both for no apparent reason. This helps your puppy know that you might do something fun when he isn't expecting it.

A game I have found particularly good with my dogs is ball play. They play with their ball all the time and always need to come back to have me throw it for them. It means when I am out with them, they rarely leave me.

Dogs can alternate between balls, sticks and even pine cones (in the winter it might be a lost glove). They might surprise you with the things they love to retrieve (I call it 'fetch' and use this word as a cue). Frisbees are also very popular with GSD's.

Giving your GSD something to find will be a game he loves. You can do this in the home and teach him the game and what you want him to find. You can start with cheese (find the cheese) and then introduce another item that you can hide outside (and old sock or t-short).

Finally, and one last example of a fun game is piggy in the middle. This is a great game for recall and everyone can join in.

As the name suggests, someone calls your puppy's name and gives them a treat or a toy, then someone else calls his name and he runs to them to get a treat or the toy, and so on. This is actually great fun and a great way to get comfortable when you go to the park for the first time.

Your puppy will let you know what games and toys he likes best.

14

LEASH AND HEEL TRAINING

Leash training is a natural partner to recall training as most of the foundations are all the same and you will have read about most of them now.

For example, your puppy will need to know his name and you will also want to train your puppy to look at you outlined in the earlier chapters.

How to hold the leash

With your puppy on the left-hand side, hold the end of the leash in your right hand with the lead across the front of your body so that you are holding the other end of the leash in your left hand, with your hand closed over the leash, palm-side down. The treats will be in your right hand.

Ideally, start with your puppy in the sit position, and say 'let's go' or pat your side and start to walk. Control him with your left hand and say the cue 'close' or 'heel' while holding a treat in front of his nose just where you want him to be.

As you change direction use something to describe the

change such as 'this way' or 'change'. Don't use 'over here' if you are using the word 'here' in another cue.

To start this training, you can also simply put him on his leash and say nothing. It is likely that when you stand still and do this, that there will be tension on the leash. As soon as the tension releases click (if you are using a clicker) and place a treat beside your foot nearest to him. Just keep repeating as tension is created and released.

The only way to get a dog to stop pulling on a leash when you are walking is to teach the heel cue.

Walking to heel

Like recall, walking to heel on or off-leash is a part of daily life and therefore this training is vital. You will want to build it into his daily training routine and do it 2 or 3 times a day for 5-10 minutes.

Heel-work training is one of those times you want to make sure your puppy is hungry so that the treats can have maximum effect and reward. You might also find that you have to retrace the training slightly more often to ensure he is always successful.

Establish the heel position

The perfect heel position is to have your puppy's head or neck in line with the knee or leg. For ease, you can use his collar as a guide.

Like all training today, you are going to show him what you want him to do, and then you are going to teach him the word that describes what he is doing.

There are two ways you can do this that I have found work well and one shows on-leash and one shows off-leash.

1. Start with your puppy in front of you with the leash

around your right-hand wrist while controlling the leash with your left hand. Place your left hand about halfway down his leash towards his collar. Hold a treat in your right hand.

Get his attention by saying his name (or using a squeaky toy) and move your left leg back a step but remain stationary. Use the treat in your right hand to encourage him towards you and into the correct position and, as you do this, move your left leg back into position.

You will encourage him to move in a semi-circle to get into the correct position. As soon as he is in the position you want, mark with a click and a treat. You can then add the signal (I use a point signal) by holding the treat in the same hand that you are using to point down by your side. Once he understands this signal, add the verbal cue heel.

2. Start with your puppy in front of you with a treat in both hands. Hold out your hand and show him the treat in your right hand and then guide him around your back until he can see the other hand with a treat in it. It is this hand (your left hand in this example), that will take him to the side of your leg and the final heel position. When he reaches the heel position praise him (or click) and give him his treat. Keep repeating until he understands the behavior.

Once you have done this a few times remove the treat from the hand that starts the movement (but keep doing the same routine) and keep the treat in the hand that guides him into the heel position. You will start to use the empty hand to create a visual cue such as pointing to the side (you can start doing this before you remove the treat).

After he has got the hang of this you can start introducing your verbal cue of 'heel'. Say 'heel' point and he should move behind you into the heel position to get his reward.

Start walking

One important tip with walking to heel is not to constantly hold the treat in front of your dog's nose. It will be tempting but it won't teach him what you need him to learn.

To build movement into his heel-work and walking, bring him to heel while stationary but don't give him the treat right away. Just bring him to heel, and then take a step forward so that he moves with you, and then reward him with his treat. Once he moves with you without hesitation move 2 steps and 3 steps and so on. Don't forget to give him lots of encouragement which will also make him want to look at you.

Every time he walks beside you in the correct position click and praise and reward and slowly build more time (and steps) between the reward. You are aiming to have him happily walking beside you in a straight line with only praise and lots of encouragement.

Once he is walking in a straight line you can then get used to changing direction. You can start to do this in lots of different ways but you can start by simply turning left or right.

Eventually, you will build in the other cues of 'this way' to change direction and his 'sit' cue. For example, you can ask him to sit after walking a few steps or before you change direction. Variations, as you move through his training, will keep him engaged especially as he starts to understand what you want him to do to get his reward.

Keep talking to your puppy and making lots of noises as you do this work - you want him to keep focused and interested in you. This will really help.

As you start walking with your puppy the leash should be relatively loose. If there is tension just stop and wait until the leash slackens then start to walk forward again. This will ensure that he can learn that there is only forward movement when the leash is slack. This works incredibly well.

Meeting other dogs while on the leash

When a dog is on a leash and he meets another dog the most likely meeting will be head-on and, as we already know, this behavior is rude in the world of dogs - and can even be seen as aggressive.

Being on a leash, by the nature of the leash-itself, makes this kind of meeting more likely, even if it is unintended by the dogs.

What you do, to try and avoid encountering this behavior, can unintentionally make things worse.

For example, if your dog is on a leash and he goes forward to another dog to say hello, and you pull him back and say 'no'.

1. This might start to create and build a negative association with other dogs.

2. If your puppy enthusiastically approaches another dog on the leash, this dog may not respond well even although they are normally friendly dogs. If this is the case, your puppy's association with other dogs might be that they are hostile and he won't understand that it was triggered by his over-enthusiastic approach. This means that he might start building a defensive reaction to other dogs.

How to greet other dogs on the leash

You need to train your puppy how to meet other dogs when they are on the leash and the best way to do this is to distract them from the other dog as they approach.

You will also want to get them used to greeting and meeting other dogs without making a fuss.

Start by training this with other dogs that he might know and then introduce dogs he doesn't know, but that that you know are friendly.

To do this with dogs that are coming towards you, use distraction until the other dog is near or has passed by. Just make sure that you are the one that gets your puppy's attention.

You are trying to get him used to other dogs approaching while on his leash without building any negative associations, and you are doing this by not allowing any situation to arise because he is focused on you, and not an approaching dog.

You will approach it like this whether he is on or off-leash but, when he is on the leash, he is going to feel more constrained and has fewer options in how he greets the oncoming dog.

The best way to do introduce your puppy to another dog while he is on the leash, and to educate him that he can do this as long as his leash is not being pulled, is to use direction change. As he starts to pull towards another dog, change direction by saying your direction change cue, for example, 'this way'. This also releases the tension on the leash.

Remember to reward him but keep moving in the direction of the other dog. If you are a sailor this might remind you of tacking. When you get there ask him for a sit. Once he is sitting you can talk to the other owner and he can greet the other dog (just make sure you know this dog is ok with this).

Advanced Training

German Shepherds like and want to work and training is a great to way to enable them to do that as well as providing great mental and physical exercise.

In this book we cover all the early puppy training but GSD's are keen - and fast - learners and they are suited to all types of training and sports.

The majority of further training will take place after his puppy phase (perhaps 18 months) and you may decide to start with obedience training. Obedience training is also used in other advanced training e.g. Agility, Detection, Tracking, Protection and Schutzhund.

Schutzhund is traditional sports training for GSD's (and

other working and protection dogs) and it focuses on tracking, obedience, and protection skills. You will need a qualified trainer and, if there is one in your area, you should join a Schutzhund club.

Don't try to train your GSD for protection by yourself. This will also require professional trainers to ensure you don't create issues with your GSD where none had previously existed

We also mention using had signals throughout the puppy training and you, and your dog, will need these skills if you do want to get involved in competition sports.

15

SEPARATION ANXIETY

It's important to understand separation anxiety because it should form a part of all puppy training.

Separation anxiety affects at least 1 in 7 dogs in the United States with some studies reporting it might be as high as 1 in 5. New Research from Finland has found that as many as 70% of our dogs are suffering from some kind of fear – and the most common is the fear of noise.

GSD's are known to be more prone to separation anxiety than other breeds so this part of your training will be especially important.

Older dogs can, and do, develop separation anxiety too, and this can be for several different reasons and it has happened to my dogs.

Separation Anxiety can be a form of separation distress or isolation distress - a milder form of separation anxiety. I use the terms separation anxiety as a general term but it will depend on the depth of the issue for your dog.

Separation anxiety happens when a dog reacts to separation (usually when their 'family' leaves the home) and this results in your dog getting stressed. This stress is released in a variety of ways, from whining and barking, to chewing and destruction with a few poops in between.

This book is not intended for those dogs with serious anxiety problems, but rather as a guide, to help with some of the basic steps to ease your and your dog's anxiety with separation - and to also explain why they feel the way they do.

Dogs are used to living with others. They are pack animals, and in nature, are never alone. As mans best friend this means their pack includes us and everyone else we may live with in our homes. In its simplest form, being 'separate' is not a natural experience for a dog.

Humans can, and do, live more separately. We are used to it because we need to do things like go to work, we might need to go to school or we just need to go shopping.

We are therefore asking our dogs to behave unnaturally. This means that we need to teach them how to live in our world where some form of separation is a necessity.

There are a few theories on why dogs react the way that they do. The most important thing to know is that if they are suffering from any degree of separation anxiety then, for one reason or another, they are getting stressed when you leave and they are being left alone.

All you need to do is to help teach them that being alone without you is not to be feared.

Not all dogs are the same

Separation or canine separation anxiety can affect all dogs. Although research suggests that dogs are more likely to develop separation behavior problems if they are male, come from a shelter, or are separated from the litter before they are 60 days old.

Interestingly dogs born at home were more likely to suffer anxiety than those born with a breeder.

Dogs that tend to have higher levels of alertness, like GSD's, are also thought to increase the chance of that dog experiencing separation anxiety.

In research, mixed breed dogs were more likely to destroy, urinate or defecate when left alone, whereas Wheaten Terriers were likely to vocalize, salivate or pant.

And where separation anxiety existed, almost all of the dogs also had a fear of noise. Miniature Schnauzers and Staffordshire Bull Terriers were the least affected by noise.

Not all dogs of the same breed will develop separation anxiety, it just means that there is a higher tendency that they might be more susceptible.

German and Australian Shepherds are believed to be more likely to suffer from this due to their high levels of vigilance, energy and loyalty.

Causes and Signs Of Separation Anxiety

Separation anxiety is not a failure on the owner's part and there can be many reasons that a dog reacts like this.

There may have been a change in ownership either from another home or from a shelter, there may have been a house move or a change in the routine of the family, it might be due to divorce or the loss of a family member (usually another dog but it could be a cat or even a family member moving away to school).

For puppy's, it might simply be the first time they have been left alone having been used to being around people all the time.

Dogs may also have had a bad experience - firecrackers, a delivery person, or the noise from trash pick-up. Dogs don't like sudden and unexpected noises.

Like anyone, dogs can get more nervous if they are alone. But remember dogs are not used to dealing with threats alone, they are used to packs who are there for safety as well as nurture.

If they are already nervous or uncomfortable then they will feel even more vulnerable when they need to deal with these 'threats' alone in their home.

Finally, dogs may be bored. Boredom usually affects young or energetic dogs who still don't know what to do when they are left to play - or relax - alone and they will seek out ways to keep themselves entertained.

Like chewing furniture - this is also a calming activity - or exploring the trash. Exercise will help with this and this is covered later.

Dogs will do some of these things some of the time. But when they display this behavior some or most of the time then it is likely your dog is suffering from some degree of separation anxiety.

Dogs will get bored when they are left alone. Your dog will sleep – dogs sleep for between to 10 to 14 hours a day - but he will be awake at various points and he will be looking for something to do.

He might have a sniff around, have a drink or two, and then look for something else to occupy his mind, his energy, and his time.

Dogs like to put things in their mouth, some things fit in their mouths and some things don't. This means that sometimes the mess you discover on returning home is simply a sign of a bored dog and not necessarily one suffering from anxiety.

This doesn't make the experience of returning home any more pleasant but exercise will help and finding toys that he can play with will relieve some of that boredom. Other signs, that are more likely to be separation anxiety, are more obvious.

The first thing I noticed was howling when I left the house. I didn't notice it - one of my neighbors told me that when the dog walker dropped them off after their walk they would howl for hours. Until this point, I had no idea.

This not only made me feel like a bad dog parent, but it also made me feel like a bad neighbor.

I would then leave the house for a few minutes and wait outside to see if this was an occasional thing or something they did all the time. Sure enough, after a few minutes, I would hear the howling.

This made it very hard for me to leave the house without worrying about them - and my neighbors. Commonly, the signs of distress manifest almost as soon as you leave the house.

Howling or barking is not the only sign of separation anxiety. Other signs are excessive barking, panting or whining, and indoor accidents. This won't be due to not being housebroken.

Stress can result in either peeing or pooping or both. They may also chew things to calm themselves, scratch at doors or windows and some might try to escape.

They are more likely to be scratching the door that you left from, or the window from where they can see you leave, they might chew something that smells of you - a shoe, sock, or even a magazine.

Signs of general stress in dogs will be panting and pacing and this may well be evident in your dog if he or she is suffering from separation anxiety.

Is your dog panting when you return home? This might be due to whining and barking while you were gone. You will notice this at other times too.

Separation anxiety is not only when you leave the house and the dog is alone. It can also be when dogs become anxious when they are not seated near you or can't see you even if you are still at home.

Does your dog follow you around and want to sit beside you all the time? Do they sit against your legs or feet (this way they will know as soon as you move)? Again, German Shepherds do like to follow you around.

What happens when you leave? Is it only you that your dog is focused on (if you share your home with family). In some cases, it doesn't matter if the dog is with another person in the home when you leave. Again, German Shepherds are often fixated on just one leader.

If you share your home and want to find this out, simply have a friend or another family member stay with your dog (with some treats) and leave the house.

How does your dog react? Do they ignore the treats and look for you and if they do, how long for? Or do they settle down with the other person and enjoy their treats?

If you are not sure how your dog is reacting when you leave then it is useful to record your dog when you are not there. What does he do when you leave? Does he go to the door for a few minutes - how long?

Take note of everything you can see and what he does. This is one of the best ways to find out what is happening when you are gone.

What to watch out for

Does your dog start to behave differently as you get ready to leave, either before you have started to get ready or when you are getting ready to leave? My dogs started to react to me picking up my coat or my car keys.

If I was going on a trip - which might only be once every few months, one of my dogs would immediately start to pace around and look 'sad' as soon as I got a suitcase out.

The first thing to do is to take notice of their behavior and try and think about if it has changed and why it might have changed. What changes have you made, if any?

Notice how much and how often your dog is following you

(even if he is a new puppy). If it's an older dog try to think back to any changes - is he sitting beside you more often, following your more than he used to? Is there any other reason or a point in time that you can identify?

The solution to this part of their behavior is to slowly build them up to being comfortable with you not being beside or near them so that they get used to your absence and learn (or re-learn) that you come back.

Sometimes any or some of the signs can be there for other reasons so if you are worried at all just check with your veterinary.

Why Punishment Won't Work

Before we talk about all the things that can be done to help with separation anxiety it is useful to understand why punishment just won't work.

Have you ever taken your dog over to the 'scene of the crime' and pointed at it. I have done this and we all will have done this.

Notice that the dog appears to look guilty and might cower. We, as humans, project our feelings or interpretation onto this behavior and assume that the dog is noticing what it has done and feels 'guilty' about it.

This is not what is happening. What we see as 'looking guilty' is appeasement behavior. It can be a way that your dog is releasing tension to try and get rid of their fear. The cowering, flat ears and tail between the legs or looking away is your dog trying to placate you.

The dog will know that she emptied the trash all over the kitchen floor and dragged some of it into other rooms but it won't connect what it has done wrong.

And he definitely won't connect something that happened 2 or 3 hours ago when you arrive home to find the mess.

All your dog will know is that you are not happy and he will pick this up from you and be fearful and will try to placate you but he won't know what he has done.

Dogs won't associate something done hours or even minutes ago with the here-and-now. No matter how much we tell them, they simply won't understand why we are angry with them - just that we are.

And this means they won't understand why they are being punished. They will only connect that you arrive home and they get punished.

This means that punishment when you return home will make your dog not only stressed about you leaving, but stressed about you coming home too. This can make any anxiety worse.

Just remember, the dog has not done this to deliberately annoy you nor to 'get back' at you. He did it because he was stressed and anxious or bored and then tried to use that pent-up energy.

Preparation and Socialization

It's a good idea to get your puppy used to being separated from you when they are young. Even if you don't expect to be away from them often, there will be times when you will need to.

Teaching your puppy not to fear this absence and to let them know that they can be relaxed when you are not there is one of the best things you can do for both your puppy, and for yourself.

If your puppy can get used to being left for short periods when they are young then they are more likely to grow up feeling relaxed and comfortable when left on their own for part of the day.

These are all really simple things to do and are obvious

once you know them. You will need to do this slowly, teaching them bit by bit over time.

The first 3 basic steps you need to take are the following ones.

1. Pick the room you want your puppy or dog to be in when you are not in the house - either in their basket, bed, or crate. Decide which room this is going to be as early as you can.

2. Once you decide on where this is, start getting them used to being in this room - don't wait until the time when you are going to leave the house.

3. Spend time with your puppy or dog in this room - you want them to understand it is not a punishment 'place' or a place that is apart from you but a part of their household.

Create a physical barrier between the room you want them to remain in and the room you are in - make this something they can see you through (like a gate).

Once you have picked the room that you want your dog to stay in when you leave the house, create a gate to the room but make it a barrier or gate so that your dog can still see you. Remember not to interact with your puppy or dog when they are there - just go about doing things as normal.

Don't forget to spend time with them in this room when you are **not** about to leave, spend time there during the day or when you are training them so that this becomes a place that you are a part of too.

As you begin their training, the first thing you will do after you have created the gate is to just be on the other side of the gate to your dog. Do this for 2 or 3 minutes but if your dog starts to get stressed just calmly let them out.

Keep building their confidence and slowly make the time longer. Start moving around and doing other things as you build up the time and distance. At this point, you will always be in sight.

If they start to get anxious just move forward or return to

the point where they were comfortable. Once they are comfortable with the distance, start to move out of sight to another room for a few minutes and then repeat the process of stretching the time. Begin by moving to the door of the room.

Then move into another room out of sight (but they will still be able to hear and smell you). Return after a few minutes, and then repeat building up the time as you go along.

Finally, go to the main door and go outside for a few minutes. Once again repeat the process of increasing the time you are away and check how your dog is reacting.

If there are signs of stress or anxiety just go back a couple of steps and begin building up your dog's confidence once again. Keep the time as short as you need to, it can start with as little as 5 or 10 seconds and build the time based on your dog's response.

From the very start let the dog know that the place you have chosen is their safe place. Keep all their things in this room and place their bed or crate in here as soon as you can along with some toys.

If you are using a crate, keep the crate door open - let them get used to going in and out of the crate and choosing to do so.

Get some chew toys for them. Chew toys are good because chewing is calming action (and it's why they chew things they shouldn't). You could also put an item of your clothing in the room so that they can more easily smell you and feel more secure.

The chew toys help your dog use their mind to try and work out how to get the food or treat removed. Giving a reason for dogs to exercise their mind keeps them busy and happily occupied.

A Kong is a great chew toy to use because, as well as the chewing, the fun of getting the treats or food out of the inside of the King exercises their mind.

Put on some sound - like a radio talk station. Not at a high volume - you only want to muffle any unexpected sounds. Whatever you choose make it something that you listen to so that they are familiar with it.

Your dog will be paying attention to any noise they hear so this can help disguise some of the day-to-day noises that might go on outside (or inside) your home. It is useful to do this as soon as you begin the training so that it becomes familiar.

Try to teach your dog not to follow you all the time in the home and get them to go to different places in the house. Test them being in a room while you are in another. Don't force this or make them feel stressed about it. You need to teach them to be comfortable with it.

Play a game where you ask them to remain in one room while you move to another, then come back. If they stay where they were, come back and give them a reward - it can be a treat or affection/well done. Once again, do this calmly because if you do, then you will keep your dog calm too.

Remember when you come back not to increase or cause excitement. This can be a great game for your dog and they will enjoy it as much as you enjoy the results of it.

When you are ready to start the next phase of actually leaving the house there a few more things you can do to keep your dog calm while you are out.

How to leave and return

Start by leaving the house for a minute, 2 minutes, 3 minutes, and so on and try and return before they are anxious. If you can, then leave for longer and build up to an hour and so on.

If you notice they are not comfortable, then go back to the point when they were, and start from there again. Build the time up again.

Aim to build the routine - perhaps a treat as you leave. But don't kiss and cuddle them and make a fuss with gestures and by your comments. Try and make it as normal and calm as possible.

Once you start leaving altogether, do so for short periods at the start, and build up the time to 2, 3 and 4 hours - and make sure they have something to play with or to eat.

Ideally, don't leave your dog alone for more than 4 hours. If you can ask a neighbor or a friend to visit - one your dog might know - or a dog walker. If you are able, come home from work for lunch.

You might start to notice that your dog starts to get anxious when you put on your shoes or coat or if you pick up keys or a bag.

If they start to react to these signs then start training them to get used to these things. Put on your shoes or coat or grab your keys but don't leave. Do something else or sit down and relax (or watch the TV). Keep doing this during the day so that they don't associate these things with your departure.

For example, one of my dogs would start jumping around as soon as I got my boots out. Initially, I put them on in another room, and then I realized I had to be in control of their reaction.

I put the boots on then didn't leave (you can do this with keys/coats etc, pick them up or put it on and just sit for a while).

You can also try body-blocking. As soon as they started to get agitated as the boots or coat come out, interrupt his behavior by standing up straight and then asking him to go to his basket.

It's important not to be angry - they aren't doing anything wrong - you just want them to do something else so let them know what that is e.g. go to their crate or their basket.

You might need to re-trace your steps a few times and go back a few paces in the separation training from time-to-time as you are building their confidence and their sense of 'normal'. Just go back to the point where your dog was last comfortable.

Take this slowly - leave and come back. Build their knowledge and confidence. Having them exercised will help reduce their energy levels so remember to make sure they have had a walk and have been fed. This will make them tired.

You can also try giving them a favorite treat. This might help them associate your departure with something they can look forward to.

Someone I know uses a hollowed-out bone with frozen dog food inside (they put the dog food in the bone then freeze it). You could do the same with a Kong..

When you return, don't get them excited with happy cries of "Hello!". Don't over-excite them or over-reward them when you come back. Just arrive home and then ignore them for 5 minutes.

You need to make the exit and return a very normal thing rather than any kind of event to be excited about.

If they have done something wrong on your return don't punish them or shout at them. They won't understand why.

Summary

- Don't make a fuss of your dog when you leave. Don't and kiss them and say 'goodbye'.
- Leave calmly.
- Give them their favorite treat as you leave - give them something to chew on.
- Make sure they have been exercised.
- Don't excite them as soon as you return home, wait a few minutes before greeting them.

(These steps were the single most effective thing that I did to help my dog with separation).

Leaving when using a crate

When you put your dog in their crate (if you use a crate) before you leave then don't close the door right away. Put them in and wait until they calm down or lie down.

This might take a few minutes or more so do something else and give them time to relax and be calm. Close and open the door a few times if you like but wait until they lie down before you close the door.

Don't bribe them into the crate with a treat and then immediately shut the door - just take your time and let them take their time to get comfortable.

Once they are comfortable in their space and their room then you can start moving away using the methods detailed in the first step.

Some other useful tips

Exercise is an important part of curing separation anxiety and it is particularly important for GSD's.

A 2015 study by PLoS One found that dogs with noise sensitivity and separation anxiety had less daily exercise.

This suggests that exercise is one of the biggest things you can do to prevent or improve separation anxiety in your dog.

You need to make sure your pet gets lots of exercise every day because a tired, happy dog will be less stressed when you leave.

The study also found that dogs that were exercised off-leash were less likely to suffer from separation anxiety or fear around noise. The likely reason for this is that being on a leash, partly on a leash, or running free has an impact on the amount of exercise a dog has.

A dog whines when it starts to get tense or excited - think of as them releasing their energy. Sometimes they whine because they want something - if this is the case, they will make it obvious what they want.

If you notice this and the reason is not obvious then try and work out why it might be excited and calm them down before the excitement level rises.

If you have multiple household members - try and share the dog equally amongst everyone - so the dog doesn't focus all their attention onto one person.

If there are more members then one can leave and he dog will worry less. Research shows that dogs in multiple person households are more likely to suffer from separation anxiety – I had expected it to be the other way around.

The 10 Steps to help Separation Anxiety

1. Create a physical barrier between the room you want them to remain in and the room you are in - make this something they can see you through.
2. Put their bedding or basket in this room along with any of their toys and the bowls.
3. Put on some sound - like a radio talk station. Not at a high volume - you only want to muffle any unexpected sounds.
4. Teach your dog not to follow you all the time in the home.
5. Don't make a fuss of your dog when you leave. Don't cuddle and kiss them and say 'goodbye'
6. Leave calmly
7. Give them their favorite treat as you leave - give them something to chew on
8. Make sure they have been exercised
9. When you return don't over-excite your dog as soon as you arrive home (if there is a mess, don't punish your dog)
10. Wait a few minutes before you acknowledge them and say hello.

16

GROOMING

German Shepherds are not known as German Shedders for nothing!. They shed - a lot - and you will want to brush your GSD every day if you can.

But, don't be tempted to clip your GSD. His double coat keeps him warm in the winers and cool in the summer and you don't want to remove the outer, water-repellent coat that also acts as a UV shield.

The first thing you need to do is invest in is a good vacuum cleaner! And then you will invest in a good deshedding tool.

DESHEDDING

Deshedding tools penetrate through to your dog's undercoat, removing loose hairs that either would have fallen from your pet naturally or contributed to tangles. A Furminator is often recommended as a good deshedding tool.

You will want to de-shed at least weekly and every 1-2 days when he is shedding more heavily (usually in Spring and the Fall). If you can, groom him outside because there will be a lot of hair released.

Diet can also play a role in the amount your GSD is shedding. If you notice a lot more shedding than normal, then you might want to change his diet (ideally to a diet of high quality protein).

Ears

GSD's can be prone to ear infections and some of them can be serious. If you notice any discomfort take him to the vet as soon as you can.

Ear infections can be dealt with quickly if the are caught early but can be very difficult to treat is the infection is established.

It means that you need to clean a GSD's ears. You can use hypoallergenic baby wipes. They tend to work well.

I have covered the ears in more detail in Chapter 3 on Health.

Teeth

You will start getting your puppy used to having something in his mouth at an early age so that be will be comfortable with you cleaning his teeth when he gets older and needs it.

Use a dog tooth brush or, if you don't have one, then you can use a child's toothbrush. You should clean his teeth at last twice a week and ideally every day.

Bathing

You really don't want to bathe your GSD more than a few times a year - twice is sufficient. Bathing can remove the natural oils from their coat and over-doing bathing can cause skin problems.

17

FAMOUS GERMAN SHEPHERDS

Here are just some of the famous German shepherds over the years from film starts to home grown hero's.

STRONGHEART (ETZEL **von Oeringen**) Born on October 1, 1917, Etzel von Oeringen was a male German Shepherd bred by private German breeder, Robert Niedhardt.

Etzel served in the German Red Cross during WW1. After the war his owner was left in poverty and he sent his much loved the dog, then aged 3, to a friend who operated a kennel in New York in order to be sold.

Etzel was seen by film director Laurence Trimble, possibly at the Shepherd Dog Club of America show in October 1920, and he persuaded Jane Murfin, the screenwriter for his movies, to buy Etzel.

Eztel's name was then changed to Strongheart at the suggestion of the PR department of First National Pictures.

Trimble had also been the owner of Jean, a Collie, and the first canine movie star, known as the Vitagraph Dog.

Trimble trained Strongheart and directed him in four movies that were scripted by Murfin between 1921 and 1925 making him the first major canine star, and preceding Rin Tin Tin.

Strongheart's films encouraged the popularity of the German Shepherd breed and he and his mate, Lady Jule, had many puppies and their line is believed to continue to this day.

In 1929, while filming a movie, Strongheart accidentally made contact with a hot studio light and was burned. These burns caused a tumour, which eventually lead to his death at Murfin's home later that year.

In the 1930's, Strongheart's popularity encouraged the Doyle Packing Company to use his name and photograph for canned dog food. It was still available until around 2002.

There are at least 5 well-known books dedicated to Strongheart, two were written by J. Allen Boone who worked for the Washington Post.

Boone looked after Strongheart when Murfin and Trimble were away and Boone was reportedly very close to him.

His 2 books, *Letters to Strongheart* (1939) and *Kinship with All Life* (1954), were about animal communication and the survival of the dog's soul after death.

RIN TIN TIN

Rin-Tin-Tin became an international movie star in the 1920s. His owner was American soldier Lee Duncan who found him in a French battlefield during World War I, and who then took him back to live with him in the United States.

His first big movie was *Where the North Begins* in around 1923. He went on to star in more than 20 other Hollywood films before passing away in 1932.

After his death he lived on in Duncan's other German Shepherds and in the television shows, *The Adventures of Rin Tin Tin* and *Katts and Dogs*.

Rin Tin Tin II would sire Rin Tin Tin IV, and both dogs were used in the filming of The Adventures of Rin Tin Tin, which first aired on ABC 1954-1959.

Both Strongheart and Rin Tin Tin have stars on the Hollywood Walk of Fame.

LONDON

The Littlest Hobo, starring a dog called London, was originally created by Dorrell McGowen for a television movie in 1958.

Following the success of the movie, a television series of 65 episodes was made between 1963 and 1965. It was remade in 1979.

GSD Hero's

NEMO

In 1965, Nemo was sent out with 40 other sentry dogs to South Vietnam in order to assist the U.S. Air Force and to detect incoming enemy movement. In 1966 enemies got past the perimeter and he and his handler, Airman 1st Class Robert Throneburg, attacked them.

Nemo was hit on the nose and lost an eye during battle. He was recognised as a hero for saving his handler's life.

LUCCA

Lucca, a German Shepherd/Belgian Malinois mix, was a service dog trained to detected explosives. She was sent to Iraq twice and once to Afghanistan and with the Marines where she involved in over 400 missions. In 2012, Lucca was injured by an IED and lost her left leg and had to retire. She was awarded a Dickin Medal from the People's Dispensary for Sick Animals and was awarded an unofficial Purple Heart plaque.

Lex

While deployed in Iraq as part of an explosive detection team for 3rd Reconnaissance Battalion, Lex and his Marine Corps handler Corporal Dustin J. Lee were caught in a rocket attack, killing Lee and severely wounding Lex. Lex refused to leave his handler's side and eventually had to be dragged away. Because of this, Lex became the first physically fit military dog to be given early retirement. He lived out the rest of his life with his former handler's family until he passed away in 2012.

Apollo

Apollo was the first search-and-rescue dog to arrive at the South Tower of the World Trade Centre on September 11, 2001. Along with his handler Peter Davis, Apollo dragged victims of the attack out of harm's way, dodging debris and flames as he worked. The tenacious animal worked 18 hours a day for weeks and, as a thank you for his efforts, received the American Kennel Club Ace award in 2001 and the Dickin Medal in 2002.

Buddy

Though Labrador Retrievers are the most common guide dogs today, the first Seeing Eye dog was actually a German shepherd named Buddy. She was trained as the first Seeing Eye dog after a young man named Morris Frank read an article about World War I veterans with guide dogs and reached out to the author, seeking assistance in finding a dog of his own. The author, dog trainer **Dorothy Harrison Eustis**, agreed to help, and together they trained Buddy as the first guide dog accessible to the average citizen, inspiring the creation of The Seeing Eye in 1929.

Zuyaqui

A Mexican German Shepherd, who's body put on display at the "Narco Museum" in Mexico. He is believed to be the dog who has captured the most drugs in Mexican police and military history.

Zenit

Zenit spent most of his life sniffing out IEDs in Afghanistan with his handler, Jose Armenta, and he was on the cover of *National Geographic*. Armenta lost both of his legs after a bomb exploded under him in 2011—but in 2012, the former Marine successfully adopted Zenit, enabling the duo to live together.

Fluffy

Fluffy was a German Shepherd who was turned over to US Special Forces by Kurdish soldiers in Iraq. The dog had been abused by the Iraqi military but became a well trained sentry dog, protecting US soldiers in Operation Iraqi Freedom. With the help of Vietnam war dog handlers, Fluffy was able to enjoy his well deserved retirement in the United States.

Nubs the Mut

Nubs was a wild stray found in Iraq along the Syrian border bonded with Marine Brian Dennis. The dog suffered a serious injury and Dennis nursed him back to health. Dennis was relocated, but Nubs was so taken with his Marine that he trekked 70 miles through the desert to find his best buddy.

New Jersey Task Force One

This team received an award for their search and rescue work during the WTC disaster. These dogs searched through burning debris, ignoring burnt paws, cuts and other obstacles to look for survivors and victims. For their efforts, the team earned induction into the Animal Hall of Fame.

The team consists of "Ana" Atlas; "Senta" Bacalaglu; "Claire" & "Blitz" Clemmo; "Chewbacca" Holmes; "Mikey" & "Osa" LoPresti; "Nutmeg" & "Sarge" Pittore; "Argus" Rolando; "Quest" Sullivan; "Piper" Whynman Owners -- Sarah Atlas; Dan Bacalaglu; Lorrie Clemmo; Alice Holmes; Laura LoPResti; Spring & Pat Pittore; Bob Rolando; Penny Sullivan; Sonny Whynman.

Pascha

Pascha was recognized for his work as a rescue dog in the Oklahoma City bombing, 1995 earthquake in Kobe, Japan, the Edison, N.J. explosion, and Hurricane Opal in Panama City, FL.

While these are great examples of nationally famous German Shepherds there are many more unsung hero's and these are just a few.

Bruno, a nine-month-old German Shepherd from Newfoundland who saved the life of eleven-year-old Donnie Skiffington who had been thrown from his bicycle into a ditch, where he lay unconscious and injured. Bruno licked Donnie's face until he regained consciousness, and began to pull him by the shirt collar towards home.

NELLIE, a six-year-old German Shepherd from Ontario traveled three kilometres back to her home to get help for 78-year-old Ken Emerson, who lay injured after his tractor had overturned and crushed his pelvis. When Nellie returned home, Mrs. Emerson realized that the strip of her husband's shirt wrapped around Nellie's collar was an S.O.S. message, and immediately sent for help.

HUSTLER, from Mirror, Alberta, was a three-year-old German Shepherd and is credited with saving the life of his owner, Debbie Inions. After a fall from her horse left Debbie seriously injured and unable to move, Hustler repeatedly fought against vicious attacks by two preying coyotes until they were discovered nine hours later.

MAUDE, from Pictou County, Nova Scotia and owned by Deborah Johnston and Bernard Chisholm, saved a three-year-old girl from drowning in the frigid waters of Pictou Harbour. Gripping the child's overalls in her teeth, Maude pulled the child out of the deep water.

AFTER GRADUATING from the Seeing Eye Program, **Orient** was placed with Bill Irwin. Orient led Irwin on an incredible trek on the complete length of the Appalachian Trail from Georgia to Maine. Profiled in Irwin's book Blind Courage, Orient faithfully and unconditionally assisted Bill Irwin for over nine years.

DAISY, from Ottawa, Ontario, saved her owner's three-year-old son, David, who had wandered into a busy intersection. Daisy pulled the child to safety, as two motorists who were watching the dog and the child in the intersection collided.

HERE ARE JUST some famous owners of German Shepherds.

MAJOR WAS Franklin D. Roosevelt's dog. This famous German Shepherd ripped the pants off of Ramsay MacDonald, the British Prime Minister. This occurred just as Britain was preparing to go to war with Germany.

CLIPPER WAS former US President John Kennedy's dog.

BLONDI, Hitler's pet. He tested the cyanide capsules he later consumed to commit suicide on her, and she died as a result.

CHAMP AND MAJOR are the pets of President Joe Biden. Champ passed away in 2021 and Major is the first shelter dog to live in the White House.

OTHER FAMOUS DOGS of the German Shepherd breed owned by celebrities include:

- Angel - Actor Chuck Norris
- Atticus - Actor Jake Gyllenhaal
- Happy - Fitness Guru Jack Lelanne
- Ork - Singer/Songwriter Amy Grant
- Orso - U.S. General H. Norman Schwarzkopf
- Prince - Actor Rudolph Valentino
- Tim - Singer/Songwriter Shania Twain

18

CONCLUSION

German Shepherds are perhaps the most intelligent of dogs. And also the most loyal. But you need to train them or you won't be allowing them to use their magnificent mind.

They also thrive on regular exercise to allow them to burn off all that excess energy. It is why recall training is so important for them - and for you.

Being able to get off-leash will burn up more energy and you can't do that until you know he is paying attention to you and will always come back when he receives his cue from you- every time. And we know that exercise also helps with separation anxiety.

As any GSD owner knows, other walkers often shy away from GSD's so training them to walk calmly beside you will help the over-reaction of other walkers.

If you don't give your GSD daily workouts, watch out. Your dog will get that energy out somehow, and most likely in ways you don't want.

If you can't commit to regular exercise then don't get a GSD.

It won't be fair on him. But if you can commit to his care and well-being then there is no better companion a family can have.

The puppy training weeks are important but I also strongly recommend taking your GSD to training classes if you can. Their high intelligence means they will learn fast and learn well and they will enjoy the stimulation of the training.

The first few weeks of having your puppy at home are both exciting and scary. However, once you can get your puppy used to his crate and going outside to pee or poop, then two of the most important aspects of his training and living with you will be completed.

Both of these will mean that your puppy can go anywhere with you but that he will also feel safe and secure when he has to stay at home when you go out.

You will soon forget all the annoying little aspects of the first early weeks when your puppy will do some very annoying things —the mouthing and chewing are maddening at the time and the house training can be annoying as well as a little messy.

I would encourage you to train recall as soon as you can. This is training that can save his life as well as enabling you to love your walks together.

Recall training encapsulates almost every element of training your puppy will need other than potty and crate training. As well as bringing in all the cues such as sit and stay and the recall cues of come and heel (for walking beside you) it keeps your puppy, and later your dog, safe.

Some of the training steps might take longer than others but try to do them and complete them at the pace that works for your puppy.

Just remember that our words mean nothing to a dog and we are teaching them both a word and an action that we want them to do. And don't forget your visual cues.

Don't give up. As you see your puppy progressing try not to settle for good enough. You want him to be as good as can be!

Good recall means that you and your dog can spend many happy hours together in parks, on beaches, in forests, and in hills and places you need to go. Don't forget to keep an eye out for him. GSD's love to sniff, and sometimes he won't be aware of dangers that he can't know about or see. For recall to work we need to be able to use it when it matters most.

Of all the things I have learned over the years, the one crucial bit of advice is to remember that your puppy and your dog only want to make you (and himself) happy. So don't punish him when he gets things wrong; he is doing his best.

Just teach him what you want him to do and let him know he is on the right track by using rewards, treats and love.

All dogs are different and some will find different aspects of the training harder. If you are getting frustrated or stuck then take your dog to training classes or to a trainer even at this early stage.

These training sessions can be invaluable and will sort out what you are doing wrong quickly.

And try not to get him over-excited when you leave or return home. It really is the best way to train your puppy and prevent anxiety—and it works.

19

LEAVE REVIEW

As an independent publisher with a small marketing budget, reviews are my livelihood on this platform. If you enjoyed this book, I'd really appreciate it if you leave your honest feedback. You can do this by clicking the link to leave a review. I love hearing from my readers, and I personally read every single review.

RESOURCES

Andrea Talenti, Dayna L. Dreger, Stefano Frattini, Michele Polli, Stefano Marelli, Alexander C. Harris, Luigi Liotta, Raffaella Cocco, Andrew N. Hogan, Daniele Bigi, Romolo Caniglia, Heidi G. Parker, Giulio Pagnacco, Elaine A. Ostrander, Paola Crepaldi. (n.d). *Studies of modern Italian dog populations reveal multiple patterns for domestic breed evolution.* Https://Onlinelibrary.Wiley.Com/. https://onlinelibrary.wiley.com/doi/10.1002/ece3.3842

Alt, K. (2020, August 14). *Am I Ready For A Dog? How To Be A Responsible Dog Owner.* Canine Journal. https://www.caninejournal.com/am-i-ready-for-a-dog

Animal Poison Control. (n.d.). The American Society for the Prevention of Cruelty to Animals® (ASPCA®). https://www.aspca.org/pet-care/animal-poison-control/people-foods-avoid-feeding-your-pets

Answer These 5 Questions to Find the Right Dog For You. (2017, November 2). American Kennel Club. https://www.akc.org/expert-advice/lifestyle/answer-5-questions-find-right-dog/

Blue Cross For Pets. (n.d.). Blue Cross For Pets. https://www.bluecross.org.uk/advice/dog

Committee on Nutrient Requirements of Dogs and Cats. (2006). *Your Dog's Nutritional Needs*. Retrieved. (2006). Https://Www.Nap.Edu. https://www.nap.edu/resource/10668/dog_nutrition_final_fix.pdf

What Size Dog Crate Do You Need? (n.d.). Cooper's Crates (www.Cooperscrates.Com). https://cooperscrates.com/pages/selecting-the-correct-kennel-size

Your Complete Guide to First-Year Puppy Vaccinations. (2021, February 5). American Kennel Club (Www.Akc.Org). https://www.akc.org/expert-advice/health/puppy-shots-complete-guide

Salonen, M., Sulkama, S., Mikkola, S. et al. *Prevalence, comorbidity, and breed differences in canine anxiety in 13,700 Finnish pet dogs. Sci Rep* 10, 2962 (2020). https://doi.org/10.1038/s41598-020-59837-z

Barbara L. Sherman, Daniel S. Mills, *Canine Anxieties and Phobias: An Update on Separation Anxiety and Noise Aversions, Veterinary Clinics of North America*: Small Animal Practice, Volume 38, Issue 5, 2008, Pages 1081-1106, ISSN 0195-5616, https://doi.org/10.1016/j.cvsm.2008.04.012

Home Alone. (n.d.). Blue Cross For Pets. https://www.bluecross.org.uk/pet-advice/home-alone-separation-anxiety-dogs

Tiira, Katriina & Lohi, Hannes. (2015). *Early Life Experiences and Exercise Associate with Canine Anxieties. PloS one.* 10. e0141907. 10.1371/journal.pone.0141907. Retrieved from https://www.researchgate.net/publication/283492761_Early_Life_Experiences_and_Exercise_Associate_with_Canine_Anxieties

Could You Spot A Puppy Farm. (n.d.). PDSA. https://www.pdsa.org.uk/taking-care-of-your-pet/looking-after-your-pet/puppies-dogs/could-you-spot-a-puppy-farm

Dog Psychology 101. (n.d.). Dog Psychology 101. https://dogpsychology101.com/

Emergency Instructions. (n.d.). Pet Poison Helpline. https://www.petpoisonhelpline.com/pet-owners/emergency/

Gabriella. (2021, January 15). *Hoe To Find A Reputable German Shepherd Breeder*. German Shepherd Corner. https://germanshepherdcorner.com/how-to-find-a-reputable-german-shepherd-breeder/

Gibeault, MSc, CPDT, S. (2021, February 3). *How To Teach Your Dog To Sit.* Https://Www.Akc.Org/. https://www.akc.org/expert-advice/training/how-to-teach-your-dog-to-sit/

Les Anges Gardiens. (n.d.). *Famous German Shepherds*. http://www.angesgardiens.ca/ANG/Famous.htm

Madson, MA, CBCC-KA, CPDT-KA, C. (2020, July 25). *How To Teach Your Dog To Come When Called*. Https://Www.Preventivevet.Com/. https://www.preventivevet.com/dogs/how-to-teach-your-dog-to-come-when-called

Mattinson, P. (2019, June 19). *Teaching A Dog To Heel In Simple Stages*. The Labrador Site. https://www.thelabradorsite.com/teaching-a-dog-to-heel/

Recall Training. (n.d.). Https://Www.Doglistener.Co.Uk. https://www.doglistener.co.uk/behavioural/recall_training.shtml

Simply Behaviour. (n.d.). *Simply Behaviour.* Http://Www.Simplybehaviour.Com/. http://www.simplybehaviour.com/

Yin, D. S. (n.d.). *Teaching Rover To Race To You In Cue.* Cattledog Publishing. https://drsophiayin.com/blog/entry/teaching_rover_to_race_to_you_on_cue/

Strongheart. (n.d.). Hollywood Walk Of Fame. https://walkoffame.com/strongheart/

Strongheart Dog Food. (n.d.). Trademarkia. https://trademark.trademarkia.com/strongheart-dog-food-74188712.html

Dan G. O'Neill, Noel R. Coulson, David B. Church And Dave C. Brodbelt. (2017). *Demography and disorders of German Shepherd Dogs under primary veterinary care in the UK*. (VetCompassTM) Canine Genetics and Epidemiology. https://link.springer.com/epdf/10.1186/s40575-017-0046-4

The Kennel Club. (n.d.). *White Swiss Shepherd Dog*. https://www.thekennelclub.org.uk/search/breeds-a-to-z/breeds/pastoral/white-swiss-shepherd-dog-imp/

Wamiz. (n.d.). *The White Swiss Shepherd Dog*. https://wamiz.co.uk/dog/breeds/39/white-swiss-shepherd-dog

PDSA. (n.d.). *German Shepherds*. https://www.pdsa.org.uk/taking-care-of-your-pet/looking-after-your-pet/puppies-dogs/large-dogs/german-shepherd

Universities Federation for Animal Welfare. (n.d.). *Genetic Welfare Problems of Companion Animals*. UFAW - Universities Federation for Animal Welfare. https://www.ufaw.org.uk/dogs/german-shepherd-degenerative-myelopathy

Adam P. Patterson , DVM , Karen L. Campbell , DVM , MS , DACVIM , DACVD. (2005, May). *Managing Anal Furunculosis in Dogs*. Internal Medicine. https://www.vetfolio.com/learn/article/managing-anal-furunculosis-in-dogs

Pannus and other German Shepherd Eye Problems. (n.d.). All Shepherd. https://www.allshepherd.com/german-shepherd-eye-problems/

John Carter. (n.d.). *Best German Shepherd Breeders (2021): 10 Places to Find German Shepherd Puppies for Sale*. BubblyPet. https://www.bubblypet.com/best-german-shepherd-breeders/

www.ingramcontent.com/pod-product-compliance
Lightning Source LLC
Chambersburg PA
CBHW021951160426
43209CB00001B/6